Writing—
A Way to Pray

Writing—
A Way to Pray

Arnold B. Cheyney

A Campion Book

Loyola University Press
Chicago

Loyola Press
3441 North Ashland Avenue
Chicago, Illinois 60657

Scripture taken from the New American Standard Bible, © 1960,
1962, 1963, 1968, 1971, 1972, 1973, 1975, 1977 by The Lockman
Foundation. Used by Permission.

Cover and interior design by Nancy Gruenke and Tammi Longsjo.
Cover photo direction by Frederick Falkenberg and Jill Salyards.
Cover photo by Sidney Pivecka.

Library of Congress Cataloging-in-Publication data

Cheyney, Arnold B.
     Writing—a way to pray/Arnold B. Cheyney
          p.   cm.
     Includes bibliographical references
     ISBN 0-8294-0813-4
     1. Prayer—Christianity. I. Title.
BV215.3'2'0248—dc20   94-24244
                                                    CIP

My heart overflows with a
  good theme;
I address my verses to the
  King;
My tongue is the pen of a
  ready writer.

Psalm 45:1

Contents

To those pastors who made a profound difference in my spiritual life during the second half of the twentieth century:

Ivar A. Frick, Jr.
Robert M. Graber
Felix R. Wagner
Luther B. Dyer
Daniel J. Yeary
Gerald G. Durham

The LORD is good to those who wait for Him,
To the person who seeks Him.

Lamentations 3:25

Preface

The purpose of *Writing—A Way to Pray* is to help those who see themselves as writers and potential writers use writing as a vehicle for prayer. Writing God's words plumbs the depths of Scripture so that one hears directly the clear voice of the Father. This prayer concept assumes that God's Word is the most consistent, viable, and certain way for him to commune with us as individuals.

Prayer methods are many: talking, crying out, meditating, praising, or waiting, to name a few. We pose: perhaps folding our hands, closing our eyes, prostrating our bodies, bending our knees, walking, or sitting quietly.

Most often we pray in images. Images fill our sense of understanding with shape and form. At other times, for example, in contemplation, our minds are unclouded by thought as we wait for inspiration in God's presence. There is no one exclusive method of prayer prescribed by Scripture; there are a variety of practices. *Writing—A Way to Pray* focuses on the Ignatian tradition, in which individuals exercise images to bring God into personal focus. *Writing,* by definition and exercise, is imaging.

Elizabeth Canham, in her book *Praying the Bible,* puts written prayer in this perspective:

> Writing in a prayer journal is a powerful way of making the connection between the written Word and its personal

relevance. Transcribing one's reflections on a Scripture passage is more than a simple recording of facts; it is a process. As thoughts are written down, new thoughts emerge and the writer enters into an inner dialogue. It is akin to the writing of a Gospel, because it is a way of expressing what the good news of God in Christ means to us. This is no second-hand story, but the Word of the living God spoken to and heard by us today. Sometimes a phrase will address us with such power we will read no further but savor it, ruminate upon it, allowing it to lodge deep in our consciousness. Our prayer will focus on this thought, and we can consciously take it with us into the day, maybe repeating it like a mantra during moments of quiet reflection (1987, 46).

Perhaps your mode of prayer, or lack of prayer, bothers you to the point of frustration. You want to experience God, but your ways of praying do not promote the steady intimacy with God that you want as your prayer-life pattern. Listen to the counsel of Willigis Jäger:

After a time not a few individuals are no longer satisfied with verbal prayers, with intellectual meditations, and feelings laboriously aroused . . . these individuals must have the courage to look for a new way of encountering God, since union with God is the real purpose of any and every religious exercise (1986, 74).

If you give the process in *Writing—A Way to Pray* an opportunity, actually frequent and deal with the approach for a few weeks, you will discover that the time you spend praying has increased dramatically, and, more important, that the amount of time you spend in quality prayer has increased proportionately.

The guiding principle dominating the arrangement of this book is *integrative reconciliation* (see Dembo 1988, 38). This means that the concepts found in these pages are not compartmentalized. The ideas interconnect, bonding together by the time you finish the book. Therefore, you can move from one section to another if you wish, without concern for having missed an area necessary to understanding a subsequent section.

Praying with with pen in hand may already be your way. If you are not praying at all, this is one way to begin. If your prayer life is unsatisfactory, you have nothing to lose, especially if you enjoy the writing process. I am confident that by the time you finish reading *Writing—A Way to Pray,* written prayer will anchor your petitions in a steadfast manner for years to come.

Let all who seek Thee
rejoice and be glad in
Thee;
And let those who love Thy
salvation say continually,
"Let God be magnified."

Psalm 70:4

1

Where I Am Coming From

You have some options as you read this book, options that authors do not normally suggest to their readers. If necessary, stop and meditate when you feel the urge. Think. Write down an opinion if you wish. Skip to another section. Take the book in sips or gulps; read at various times of the day or night. Leave it for a time—it will still be around. You do not need to read the entire book at once to get what you want. When you have found something of value that you can put to use, do it. Or, just read the book through in one sitting. It is short, by design, so that you will have more time for important things—such as prayer, writing, and thinking.

Thinking

I learned a valuable lesson as a graduate student at The Ohio State University in the early 1960s. A professor of higher education encouraged our class to turn him off from time to time during his lectures. He gave us a chance, during class, to simply sit and think about a point or notion that was just expressed. I welcomed the opportunity, but was skeptical of the method as a teaching tool. Drop out of a lecture to think? Come back in at my leisure? Would I miss something that might appear on a future exam? However, I tried it and passed the course with an A.

I took advantage of the time to think during class, for I was constantly studying and cramming. When a unique thought fascinated me, I turned the professor off as easily as a light switch. What a marvelous experience to think in the intellectual seclusion of a classroom! I once read that Albert Einstein had the same kind of opportunity as a professor. If a solution to a problem invaded his consciousness while he was teaching, he had the prerogative of dropping out of the class for a few days and, in seclusion, taking time to meditate on the solution.

The offer to pause and think is yours to accept or reject as you explore the passages in *Writing—A Way to Pray*. It is as easy as inserting a bookmark or a finger in this text and thinking about what you are reading.

Writing promotes thinking, as you will often read in these pages. William Zinsser explains: "Writing is thinking on paper. Anyone who thinks clearly should be able to write clearly about any subject at all" (1988, 11). Similarly, prayer writing promotes thinking prayer. "It is written, 'Man shall not live on bread alone, but on every word that proceeds out of the mouth of God'" (Mt 4:4). There is a lot to think about in the Bible—*every* word. Words like *a, the,* and *said* have importance in equal measure to beguiling and enticing words such as *supplication, oracles, precepts,* and *testimonies*.

Moreover, there are many sentences, paragraphs, chapters, and books in the Bible that stress the importance of words. Luke, a physician and the writer of the Gospel of Luke, took great pains when writing to Theophilus to let him know that what he wrote was true: "it seemed fitting for me as well, having investigated everything carefully from the beginning, to *write* [emphasis added] it out for you in consecutive order, most excellent Theophilus; so that you might know the exact truth about the things you have been taught" (Lk 1:3–4).

Similarly, Peter emphasized the veracity of the Word of God when he wrote, "for no prophecy was ever made by an act of human will, but men moved by the Holy Spirit spoke from God" (2 Pt 1:21). God's Word is trustworthy.

Writing

Some years ago, one of Maria Montessori's resourceful ideas impressed me. Montessori was the first woman to receive a medical degree in Italy. She created the *Casa dei Bambini*, or "The Children's House," in the slums of Rome early in the twentieth century. Intrigued by the methods of the psychologists Edward Séguin and Jean-Marie Gaspard Itard, she went to phenomenal lengths to fully comprehend their ideas. Their thoughts would form the philosophical structure of Montessori's program of education. She wrote:

> I did a thing which I had not done before, and which perhaps few students have been willing to do, I translated into Italian and *copied out with my own hand, the writings of these men* [emphasis added], from beginning to end, making for myself books as the old Benedictines used to do before the diffusion of printing.
>
> I chose to do this by hand, in order that I might have time to weigh the sense of each word, and to read, in truth, the *spirit* of the author (1967, 41).

That is exactly what Christians should be doing—reading the Scriptures in the *spirit* of the author!

Becoming preoccupied with any prayer method, of course, is absurd. Within a short span of time the prayer becomes an ordeal. We must be comfortable with our mode of prayer or we will never bring ourselves into consistent intimacy with the Father. Ann and Barry Ulanov write:

> If we are attentive enough, we will find patterns of prayer and develop our own discipline. We will find our own way to converse with God, drawn instead of pushed, willing what we do, not forced by a sense of duty, not stuck for words or puzzled for method. The way is only the way and not the destination, only a means and never an end (1982, 107–8).

If you are not praying, writing is one way to begin, especially if you enjoy the writing process. Or, it may be a way to change the way you are presently praying and begin again.

Time

You do not have time to pray? Then, *make* time (see application M). I choose to pray in the early morning when I am fresh. Of course, this is not possible for everyone. For Jesus, it was: "And in the early morning, while it was still dark, He arose and went out and departed to a lonely place, and was praying there" (Mk 1:35). Richard J. Foster describes Jesus' prayer schedule as "a pattern of life more than a single event" (1992, 101). We can do no less.

Dick Eastman, in *The Hour That Changes the World,* suggests a one-hour program made up of twelve five-minute prayer periods: praise, waiting, confession, scripture praying, watching, intercession, petition, thanksgiving, singing, meditation, listening, and back to praise (1978, 10). Jesus implies that an hour a day is the least one should pray. He pointedly asked Peter and the other disciples in the garden, "So, you men could not keep watch with Me for one hour?" (Mt 26:40). Is he questioning you, too?

Lack of time for prayer stymied me until I found perspective one day in the simple maxim, "You have all the time there is, there is no more." I taped it on my office filing cabinet. Time is the only thing that we all have. Even if we have no money, no obvious talent, and no ability, we still have time, the most precious commodity a person can possess. Eastman points out that "only an act of the will is required to pray" (1978, 11). This statement is probably the most succinct appraisal of why we do not pray, even during the time we do have.

Motive

Your motive for praying is extremely important. If your motive is to pray so God will send you, by special prayer-delivery, a poem, article, or novel—forget it. Prayer writing is not a short-cut to publication. Publication takes time and study and persistence. Thomas Merton has an interesting challenge for the writer and would-be writer:

> If you write for God you will reach many men and bring them joy.
>
> If you write for men—you may make some money and you may give someone a little joy and you may make a noise in the world, for a little while.
>
> If you write only for yourself you can read what you yourself have written and after ten minutes you will be so disgusted you will wish that you were dead (1961, 111).

Sitting in God's presence, allowing him to cultivate our spirituality and restructure our personality—this must be our earnest endeavor. Attempting to find writing inspiration in the spiritual atmosphere of prayer falls short of what God wishes for us. If you love reading the Scriptures, if you treasure the Word in its truth and its life-changing possibilities, and if writing is a passion within you, write joyfully into a life of prayer! For "writing in concert with reading uniquely sponsors thought and imagination" (Emig 1983, 177).

Throughout this process of entering into a deeper relationship with Christ in prayer, you must constantly ask him to teach you "good discernment and knowledge" (Ps 119:66), especially when dealing with an area such as the imagination. Hunt and McMahon counsel that

> "Visualization" and "guided imagery" have long been recognized by sorcerers of all kinds as the most powerful and effective methodology for contacting the spirit world in order to acquire supernatural power, knowledge, and healing. Such methods are neither taught nor practiced in the Bible as helps to faith or prayer. Those who attempt to do so are not following the leading of the Holy Spirit or the Word of God, but are practicing an ancient occultic technique. Legitimate uses of the imagination would involve such things as seeing mental images of something being described in a book; designing, planning, or rehearsing something in our minds; or remembering a

place or event. Such mental processes are normal aids to everyday activities and do not involve an attempt to create or control reality through mind-powers (1985, 123).

Benefits

Only a practicing writer knows the peculiar benefits of the writing experience. For example, living with a fictional character over several months brings that character into an actuality that others can only know on a lesser plane. When honest characterization achieves itself in a novel, readers are disappointed at having to finish the book because they will not be able to live with the character anymore, even though the character was pure fantasy. The writer feels an even deeper loss. This sensation is frequently the reason for more than one sequel—the need to reestablish a previous fantasy relationship.

Writing about one's problems has a therapeutic effect. At the present time, most evidence on the curative effects of writing on a person is anecdotal and not absolutely, scientifically verifiable. You may have heard people say, or even said yourself, "After that despicable act I just sat and wrote ———— a letter. I really let ———— have it. Then I tore up the letter. But I feel better about the whole situation now. I had to get it off my chest." Diaries, a poor man's psychiatrist, have served a similar purpose for many people over the years.

At Southern Methodist University, students gave samples of blood before and after writing about traumatic events in their lives. The subjects were given the following directions:

> During each of the four writing days, I want you to write about the most traumatic and upsetting experiences of your entire life. You can write on different topics each day or on the same topic for all four days. The important thing is that you write about your deepest thoughts and feelings. Ideally, whatever you write about should deal with an event or experience that you have not talked with others about in detail (Pennebaker, Kiecolt-Glaser, and Glaser 1988, 240).

The researchers found evidence that writing positively affected the students' immune response (white cells fighting off bacteria and viruses). The immunity to illness continued for six weeks. While there are disadvantages to writing about one's traumas, rather than merely talking about them, the researchers concluded that "writing is tremendously cost-effective, allows people to confront traumas at their own rates, and encourages them to devise their own meaning and solutions to their problems. Above all, writing may provide an alternative form of preventive therapy that can be valuable for individuals who otherwise would not enter therapy" (ibid., 245).

In the Bible, writing about one's problems may have been the key to David's success at keeping his sanity, for he wrote many psalms under the duress of Saul's continual hounding and his enemies' constant challenges. The verses to the old hymn *Tell It to Jesus,* written by Edmund S. Lorenz in 1876, come to mind:

> Are you weary, are you heavy hearted?
> Tell it to Jesus,
> Tell it to Jesus,
> Are you grieving over joys departed?
> Tell it to Jesus alone.

After reading Lorenz' stirring words, you just might want to *write* to Jesus! (See applications O and P.)

A report in *Psychology Today* says researchers found "active Christian" college students "having fewer colds, headaches, ulcers, respiratory problems and other ailments" than students who did not have a viable prayer life. These students "are also more likely to pray" than those who are not active in Christian circles. The researchers note "that prayer has been found to reduce tension, and it is also a means of seeking control over a situation, providing that all-important elixir: hope" (Bozzi 1988). Thomas Merton advises, "Learn how to meditate on paper. Drawing and writing are forms of meditation" (1961, 216).

Theme

The underlying theme of *Writing—A Way to Pray* is that God reveals himself through his Word more often and more consistently than in any other way. We should not depend on our own imagination, our power of visualization, or our personal inspiration as writers. Belief in the Word of God is our only hope. Belief found through the Holy Scripture is our ultimate assurance of a relational experience with the Father, Son, and Holy Spirit. Belief in the Word of God keeps us from error, "For the word of God is living and active and sharper than any two-edged sword, and piercing as far as the division of soul and spirit, of both joints and marrow, and able to judge the thoughts and intentions of the heart" (Heb 4:12).

Therefore, reach out to God through his Word and give him entrance into your thoughts.

> My son, keep my words,
> And treasure my commandments within you.
> Keep my commandments and live,
> And my teaching as the apple of your eye.
> Bind them on your fingers;
> *Write* [emphasis added] them on the tablet of your heart (Prv 7:1–3).

O God, Thou art my God; I shall seek Thee earnestly; My soul thirsts for Thee, my flesh yearns for Thee, In a dry and weary land where there is no water.

Psalm 63:1

2

Why Written Prayer?

Perhaps the best motivation for written prayer is that God too is a writer. He beckoned Moses, "Come up to Me on the mountain and remain there, and I will give you the stone tablets with the law and the commandment which I have written for their instruction" (Ex 24:12). Later, after God finished speaking to Moses on Mount Sinai, "He gave Moses the two tablets of the testimony, tablets of stone, written by the finger of God" (Ex 31:18).

Perhaps the most extraordinary lines ever written are God's words to Belshazzar. In the midst of a great feast the words appeared:

Suddenly the fingers of a man's hand emerged and began writing opposite the lampstand on the plaster of the wall of the king's palace, and the king saw the back of the hand that did the writing. Then the king's face grew pale, and his thoughts alarmed him; and his hip joints went slack, and his knees began knocking together (Dn 5:5–6).

Later in the story, Daniel interprets the writing of the hand of God, and Belshazzar learns his fate.

Christ often referred to written Scriptures, and one could assume that he wrote because he preached in the synagogues. In one situation, Christ enlightened others when, with his finger, he wrote in the dirt. The scribes and Pharisees wanted Jesus to cast the judgment of death on a woman caught in the act of adultery.

But Jesus stooped down, and with His finger wrote on the ground. But when they persisted in asking Him, He straightened up, and said to them, "He who is without sin among you, let him be the first to throw a stone at her." And again He stooped down, and wrote on the ground (Jn 8:6–8).

Perhaps Jesus took his time in the act of writing on the ground to focus the thoughts of the assembled people on what he had just said. Writing does focus one's thoughts. It also fixes thoughts so that they are not likely to wander. John wrote, "And these things we write, so that our joy may be made complete" (1 Jn 1:4). There is joy in writing and delight in the reading of writing. Writing is another way of moving into wholeness.

Pray-Write

One edge of our praying is oral: we cry, we intercede, we praise God. The other edge of prayer is silent: we watch, we wait, we listen. However, these are not the only means of maintaining contact with God. Another is to write; we can write our thoughts about God as he dictates his message to us. God tells us, "I have put My words in your mouth. . . ." (Is 51:16). Jesus attested to this phenomenon when he said, "I do not speak on My own initiative, but the Father abiding in Me does His works" (Jn 14:10). Through writing we come into an intimacy in our prayer life that searches the unfathomable depths of God's mercy and righteousness (see application F).

A corollary to writing as a prayer form is study. Leonard Boase makes an interesting observation in his book *The Prayer of Faith:* "But it should be remembered that even

study, whether it is the study of divine things or not, can become prayer . . . if it is an action done for the glory of God
and offered to Him by a right intention" (1985, 24). Paul
makes this point in more than one instance: "And whatever
you do in word or deed, do all in the name of the Lord Jesus,
giving thanks through Him to God the Father" (Col 3:17; see
also 2 Cor 10:31). Eating, drinking, studying, and writing are
each a form of prayer when done "heartily, as for the Lord"
(Col 3:23).

The last twenty years have brought a shift in the teaching
of writing—from learning to write, to writing to learn. In the
past, learning to write meant the following: instruction in the
standard procedures of penmanship; learning the parts of
speech as discrete units; diagramming sentences; constructing
declarative and interrogative sentences; devising narrative, de-
scriptive, expository, or persuasive paragraphs; and constructing paragraphs of comparison and contrast. Through these
instructional procedures a student would, with hope, learn to
construct a five-paragraph theme.

In his book *Writing to Learn,* William Zinsser proposes a
contrasting approach to writing:

> Writing organizes and clarifies our thoughts. Writing is
> how we think our way into a subject and make it our
> own. Writing enables us to find out what we know—and
> what we don't know—about whatever we're trying to
> learn. Putting an idea into written words is like defrost-
> ing the windshield: The idea, so vague out there in the
> murk, slowly begins to gather itself into a sensible shape
> (1988, 16).

Zinsser puts more emphasis on creating meaning and less
on the pragmatics of correct grammatical construction. It is
not enough to think *about* the ideas of language; we must
think *with* the ideas of language. In the same regard, it is not
enough to think *about* the ideas found in Scripture, we must
think *with* the ideas of Scripture.

Consistent fellowship with the Father in prayer is, at times,
difficult to maintain. Verbalizing a prayer is not difficult. We
open our mouths and talk to God. In times of great peril the

words come easily. There is, of course, more to prayer than calling out to God when we are in distress. Authentic prayer means developing a conscious relationship with the Father, and he with us, his children. (For an insightful discussion of prayer as a conscious relationship see Barry 1987.) Prayer is interplay, a meshing of God's thoughts with ours. Many find this conception of prayer too demanding to carry forward. Prayer is not just taking turns when speaking with God. It is a developing, merging, fusing relationship, akin to falling in love: two beings growing in unity so that the conscious relationship extends beyond the moments spent together in seclusion. William A. Barry states it this way:

> The best way to get to know Jesus is to ask him to reveal himself and then to read a gospel passage and let it stimulate our imaginations. If we do this over time, we gradually will get to know what Jesus is like, what he values and loves and what he hates. . . . As Jesus becomes more and more a real person of flesh and blood to us, we also become more and more aware of the many ways we relate to him (1987, 25).

When the consciousness of God continues with us into our everyday activities, we "pray without ceasing" (1 Thes 5:17). However, we must spend a specific period of time in prayer before we can expect to spend the rest of the day with God. Prayers wedged between appointments, finalized with abruptness, and neglected with frequency need cultivating and fertilizing.

The first step: learning to pray. The second step: praying to learn. Written prayer offers the supplicant the opportunity to learn through the process of praying.

Written Prayer

Obviously, we can do nothing of worth without God's help or consideration. Language came first from him. According to biblical chronology, God first spoke with the words, "Then God said . . ." (Gn 1:3). Later, God uttered, "Let Us make man in Our image, according to Our likeness. . . ." (Gn 1:26).

Some of the first words spoken by men and women were the names given to the beasts of the field and the birds of the sky (Gn 2:19–20).

The first evidence of writing in Scripture is the Lord saying to Moses, "Write this in a book as a memorial, and recite it to Joshua. . . ." (Ex 17:14). Later, God speaks again to Moses, emphasizing the status of writing, "Come up to Me on the mountain and remain there, and I will give you the stone tablets with the law and the commandment which I have *written* [emphasis added] for their instruction" (Ex 24:12).

God often says through his Word that he created us, that he does things for us, that he is the maker of all, and that he fights our battles for us (see application D). Therefore, God gives us language—both spoken and written. The making of language is his doing. Just as the psalmist prophesied that Jesus was the chief cornerstone, so we also say, "This is the LORD's doing; It is marvelous in our eyes" (Ps 118:23).

Again, consider the fact that prayer is dependent on language. As God creates the language of prayer in us, we learn about God. This is especially true as we allow God to speak to us in our inner room or closet (see Mt 6:6). We speak and write his thoughts, and they become our prayer. Jesus himself spoke not on his own initiative, as he readily admitted (see Jn 12:49 and 14:10). We are not as apt to use meaningless repetition if we allow God to speak through us (see Mt 6:7).

Why write? Because "He who sits on the throne said, 'Behold, I am making all things new.' And He said, 'Write, for these words are faithful and true'" (Rv 21:5).

Learning Information

Prayer writing helps us learn information. Writing God's Word requires deliberate thinking. Writers must slow their thought processes and consider what God wants them to know. Langer and Applebee conclude in their study that an understanding of the role of writing depends on the learner's ability to manipulate content, and "the more that content is manipulated, the more likely it is to be remembered and understood. In general, any kind of written response leads to better performance than does reading without writing" (1987, 130).

Joshua made sure that when he sent men through the promised land, they came back with an accurate description. They had to write down what they saw and bring it back to him.

> Provide for yourselves three men from each tribe that I may send them, and that they may arise and walk through the land and write a description of it according to their inheritance; then they shall return to me. . . . And you shall describe the land in seven divisions, and bring the description here to me (Jos 18:4, 6).

Written language is created to be read. So the question arises, what do the printed symbols (whether carved in stone or made with ink) mean? For if these symbols are in a language foreign to the reader, then there is no meaning to the person searching for a message. Therefore, meaning comes from the reader, not the symbolic representation of the message. This is especially true of the Holy Scriptures. They are not there for private interpretation. Peter said, "But know this first of all, that no prophecy of Scripture is a matter of one's own interpretation, for no prophecy was ever made by an act of human will, but men moved by the Holy Spirit spoke from God" (2 Pt 1:20–21).

Children learn to read in the primary years of elementary school. They begin haltingly but progress to some degree of proficiency. If they have not experienced or absorbed word meanings, the teacher quickly decides whether their comprehension is adequate to the task of reading. They may have only called out sounds that stood for those visual representations. From an adult standpoint, words in Scripture, such as *cost* and *sacrifice,* can have disparate meanings to persons on welfare and those who possess great wealth.

Reading Defined

We are in need, then, of a definition of *reading* as it pertains to the written word. From my viewpoint, reading is the ability to bring meaning to the printed page. There is no inherent meaning on the pages of books or magazines, in letters, or on computer screens. Meaning is a function of the reader's mind; just as beauty is not in an object but in the eye (mind) of the beholder.

When Christians read the Scriptures, they are often apt to say, "I've read that passage many times, but I never really saw it in this way." Another dimension then comes into play: the Spirit of God dwelling in the believer. The Spirit generates meaning in the mind of the Christian. It is possible to comprehend the Scriptures factually, recite the names of the apostles, memorize Psalm 23, or discuss intelligently the three missionary journeys of Paul, and still not *know* experientially the meaning and purpose of God's word to humankind. Worse yet, a person may not know the intimacy of the Christ of Scripture.

Thinking God's Thoughts

Prayer writing helps us think more profoundly. As we write our thoughts during prayer, our minds remain active and are not likely to falter in the prayer process. The message in prayer does not veer from its objective. The psalmist muses: "Deep calls to deep at the sound of Thy waterfalls. . . ." (Ps 42:7). God's waterfalls are refreshing, cleansing, profound. His depths call to our depths. Thinking *about* God, thinking *with* God, thinking *in* God with writing brings an additional dimension to prayer. Prayer is a process; it is not fixed, static. It is on a continuous loop, never returning to "Me [God] empty" (Is 55:11).

For those who have been writers for any length of time, the phenomena of the subconscious working in elusive ways during the night are not only mysterious but also exhilarating. The experience of sleeping on a troublesome problem and receiving a solution at dawn is common. David tells us we should bless the Lord for this occurrence: "I will bless the Lord who has counseled me; Indeed, my mind instructs me in the night" (Ps 16:7). And later he declares: "Day to day pours forth speech, And night to night reveals knowledge" (Ps 19:2).

Zinsser defines the subconscious mind in this fashion:

Your subconscious mind does more writing than you think. Often you will spend a whole day trying to fight

your way out of some verbal thicket in which you seem
to be tangled beyond salvation. Surprisingly often a solution will occur to you the next morning when you
plunge back in. While you slept, your writer's mind
didn't. To some extent a writer is always working. Stay
alert to the currents around you. Much of what you see
and hear will come back, having percolated for days or
even months through your subconscious mind, just when
your conscious mind, laboring over the typewriter, needs
it (1980, 112).

We inform ourselves when writing. We inform ourselves
about God's will for us when we pray and anticipate words running—and pouring forth—from our pens as we "address [our]
verses to the King" (Ps 45:1). The King, in turn, informs and
sets in motion for us his own battle strategy (see application D).

Shaping God's Meaning

God's meaning shapes us with the words we write. The shape
of that meaning is not set in stone, as the Ten Commandments. It is there for recollection, change, deletion of our own
sin, imprudence, and mistakes, awaiting the perfection of a
righteous God. Just as revision of written material is standard
procedure for shaping and forming the meaning of our written words in secular work, so does revision of prayer attempt
to see whether we have captured the essence of God's
thoughts and integrated ours with his. Are the now visible
thoughts correct or are they in need of the purifying, cleansing, and shaping hand of God?

Writing shapes thinking. As we fashion words into sentences they take on life in our minds. They generate new
thoughts, which shape the contours of our reflections and the
avenues of our mind processes. Writing designs thoughts.

At the same time, thinking shapes meaning. Ann Berthoff
distinguishes between *message* and *meaning*. She points out
that reading for message is different from reading for meaning. The word *message* possibly calls to our attention a list of
grocery items we are to get before returning home. The word
meaning may transform the grocery list into the personifica-
tion of who will appear at the dinner table for the evening

meal. Messages tell. Meanings explore messages. Meaning is like mercury, slipping away and manifesting itself to others or even to ourselves at another time. Berthoff explains:

> Meanings are not things, and finding them is not like going on an Easter egg hunt. Meanings are relationships: they are unstable, shifting, dynamic; they do not stay still nor can we prove the authenticity or the validity of one or another meaning that we find. But that does not imply a necessary solipsism; it doesn't mean that the only thing we can say is "To me it means X—and that's that!" (1981, 42).

We must nurture the mental attitude that our interpretations, while imperfect, are leading to a livelier understanding of God's nature in us. While Christ enjoins us "to be perfect, as your heavenly Father is perfect" (Mt 5:48), we realize that our journey is one in which we need his guiding hand upon us constantly.

Thinking Flexibly

Writing stimulates flexibility of thinking. God needs Christians with flexibility in their thinking: looking at fundamental truths in creative ways and applying them to the time in which we live without losing their essence or the basic values that they represent. Thinking flexibly enhances writing because the ideas are visible before a person and, consequently, more adaptable to revision. On the other hand, spoken words vanish the moment they are uttered, unless they are electronically transcribed.

The ultimate in thinking flexibly is to think God's thoughts. Reflect on this verse from Jeremiah in the King James translation:

> For I know the thoughts that I *think toward you* [emphasis added], saith the Lord, thoughts of peace, and not of evil, to give you an expected end (Jer 29:11).

Integrating Information

Writing integrates information. There is no integration of information on a blank page. When writing is on a page, it is more likely to be associated with the other thoughts that are going to be placed there. Integration is a process the reader instigates. This is especially true in the double-entry notebook where the words of the Scripture writer are in the left column juxtaposed with the thoughts of the reader/reactor in the right column (see application H). The integration of the material is at once available for reflection and exchange.

Engaging Complex Thoughts

Writing engages complex thoughts. The brain, with all its circuitry, is an immensely sophisticated machine. Explosions of thought sweep across the contour of our gray matter, merging and breaking in upon one another. Through practice these thoughts energize themselves. We need to see them as manipulable entities on paper. "And when information is manipulated in more complex ways, it tends to be better understood and better remembered" (Langer and Applebee 1987, 136).

Most of us need all the help we can get. The complex thoughts we find in Scripture come at us in a variety of writing styles, written by many authors over several hundreds of years. There are genealogies, laws, parables, poems, proverbs, prophecies, psalms, stories, histories, and letters, to name a few. To make sense of all this takes more than just a clear mind, it takes enhancement and discernment given by the Holy Spirit to help us in our understanding.

Enabling Learning

Writing enables learning. Learning involves changes that occur in the thoughts and behavior of an individual; learning is the result of experience and training. By putting pen to paper, a person begins to think, and behavior changes as the writing experience progresses across the page from the core of the mind. Writing enables us to pray. Prayer enables us to love God.

Listen to David: "All this . . . the Lord made me understand in *writing* [emphasis added] by His hand upon me, all the details of this pattern" (1 Chr 28:19). The following examples illustrate what David learned through writing with God's hand upon him (1 Chr 28:11–18):

1. The pattern of the temple, including the porch, the rooms, and the building itself

2. The pattern for the courts of the house of the Lord

3. The plan for the divisions of the priests and the Levites

4. The weight of the gold and silver to be used in all utensils, lampstands, basins, pitchers, bowls, and so on

5. The weight of the gold for the altar and the model of the chariot and cherubim

David had to be "enabled" for he could not remember all the information and, interestingly, the Lord used writing to do it.

Focusing Learning

Writing keeps a person focused. Written words remind us to think immediately, while memory is often fleeting. Proverbs tells us:

> Have I not written to you excellent things
> Of counsels and knowledge,
> To make you know the certainty of the words of truth
> That you may correctly answer to him who sent you?
> (Prv 22:20–21).

Prayer writing brings the senses—such as touch, hearing, and sight—to bear on the prayer process. This sensory modality, a type of learning style, is how many people interact with their world, that is, how they best learn. The actual putting of pen to paper (touch), listening for God to speak (hearing), and viewing the written symbols (sight)—for example, a quote from Scripture and the person's subsequent written reaction to it—are aids to experiencing prayer with the Father.

There are many ways of using writing during prayer time. One of the first things to remember is that your writing does not have to be perfect in terms of spelling, punctuation, or grammar. Chances are that no one but yourself will see what you have written. The main idea, as you read Scripture, is to do focused free-writing on whatever comes to mind as you meditate on God's Word. This method of spiritual communication can be done in many ways and will be the subject of the next two chapters. After all, the words from our mouths and the meditation from our hearts are what matter most.

> Let the words of my mouth and the meditation of
>   my heart
> Be acceptable in Thy sight,
> O Lord, my rock and my Redeemer (Ps 19:14).

Seek the L<small>ORD</small> and His
strength;
Seek His face continually.

Psalm 105:4

3

Types of Written Prayer

Oliver Wendell Holmes, Jr., wrote, "We too need education in the obvious—to learn to transcend our own convictions" (Bartlett 1968, 787b). After reading the suggestions in this chapter for writing prayer, you might question the wisdom of proffering such obvious techniques. The reason is that their conspicuousness blinds us to their possibilities. But we must start somewhere. This area may be the best place for you to begin, if, that is, you are ready to take "every thought captive to the obedience of Christ" (2 Cor 10:5).

Focused Free-Writing

Macrorie says that "All good writers speak in honest voices and tell the truth" (1984, 14). He goes on to declare that writing freely with focus "involves no pressure on you. It never requires perfection. If you goof, you have not lost the game or produced a work disgraceful in the public eye" (ibid., 20). Writing freely with focus begins with a truth (focus) taken from a Scripture passage; and then you run with it. (Do not confuse focused free-writing with stream of consciousness. The latter is a method that displays the thoughts, feelings, and memories that swirl through a character's mind. For an example of stream of consciousness see *Ulysses* by James Joyce.) In focused free-writing, the nerves carry the message to the sheet of paper and the writer's hand produces the graphic record. David must have experienced the freedom to write easily with focus for he said, "My tongue is the pen of a ready writer" (Ps 45:1).

Focused free-writing procedures are the basis for most of the suggested activities in *Writing—A Way to Pray*.

Lingering Writing

Simple acts are often the most profound statements we make in life. Select a portion of Scripture. Read the passage prayerfully and then copy it verbatim in a notebook or on a sheet of paper. Think-pray as you write the words. Linger over the words. Savor them. Write a verse or paragraph and then reread what you have written before you go on to the next passage. Because this is your own writing, you need not feel concerned about underlining portions, circling others, or drawing them together with lines and arrows. At this point it may be helpful to mark portions with a highlighter or colored felt pens. They flow easily across a page and accent ideas that might otherwise lie dormant.

If pronouns make up a great portion of the text, write their antecedents in the appropriate places, especially if they are the personal *I, me,* and *you* (see application E).

Sometimes during scriptural prayer time (see application A), I linger-write with only one passage of Scripture every day of the week, such as Mark 14:3–9. In this passage, a woman comes to Jesus as he reclines at dinner. She break opens an alabaster vial and pours the expensive perfume it contains over his head. Although rebuked by some people for wasting the perfume, Jesus comes to her defense and utters these classic words: "She has done what she could." That particular truth intrigues me as I think about what I do to magnify the kingdom.

By praying-writing that passage from different biblical versions for seven days, analyzing it, underlining it, and making it part of my life, I find it becomes my prayer during the day when I am not in the conventional mode of prayer. This experience is particularly fulfilling when one has the problem of trying to find a specific time of day for prayer (see application M).

Praying by the Book

In the 1920s a phrase came into American usage: "go by the book." It means: to abide strictly—even if unreasonably so—to the rules and regulations (Partridge 1984, 474). Bureaucrats, police, and others are prone to use the concept when accused of not living up to public expectations. We, too, should follow this idea when we "pray by the book."

Some time ago, when I was in prayer, a portion of Psalm 119 made me pause for a moment. I asked myself, was I strictly "praying by the book"? Here is the passage:

I rise before dawn and cry for help;
I wait for Thy words.
My eyes anticipate the night watches,
That I may meditate on Thy word.
Hear my voice according to Thy lovingkindness;
Revive me, O Lord, according to Thine ordinances
(Ps 119:147–49).

I rose before dawn for prayer. I waited for God's word to speak to me. But my eyes did not anticipate with holiness the "night watches." I was not meditating on the Word during the night. So I asked the Lord for guidance to revive this aspect of my prayer life. When I was hospitalized for a few days, my pastor paid me a visit and we talked about prayer in the night watches.

Maintaining proper balance in my spiritual life meant replacing time usually spent watching television news programs with meditation on spiritual writings and Holy Scripture before sleep took over. I found Isaiah 43:1 especially helpful as contemplation: "Do not fear, for I have redeemed you; I have called you by name; you are Mine!"

Write, slowly, a Scripture passage. Then write your interpretation of what the passage means for you at this point in your life. Or, rewrite a passage, such as a psalm, in your own words. Go by "the book." Your days will be better, and so will your nights, "For He gives to His beloved even in His sleep" (Ps 127:2). (See application I.)

Twenty Insights

Scripture abounds with verses from which a person can receive a multitude of insights. Consider the first words of John 3:16: "For God so loved the world. . . ." What meanings come to your mind? List as many as you can. Think-pray with me: (1) God loves, (2) God loved in the past, (3) God loves inclusively, that is, everyone, (4) God loves the world he created, and so on. Remember the words of Jesus in an earlier chapter: "Man shall not live on bread alone, but on *every* [emphasis added] word that proceeds out of the mouth of God" (Mt 4:4).

This prayer writing exercise pulls a person into the deep recesses of God's heart. It requires thoughtful and persistent prayer. A study Bible can be of major help. Read the sidebar references to Scripture passages and you will find many insights. See application G for a verse with which to begin. Then, after you have listed twenty insights, put the paper aside and find an additional twenty the next day. Impossible? Not at all.

Know, Think, Wonder

As you pray through Scripture passages, stop from time to time and reflect by writing from a prompt: I know, I think, or I wonder.

The first prompt, "I know," is an answer from the experience of your life. It is not so much an act of faith but a certainty based on knowledge gained through experience. The word *know* is used 911 times throughout the Bible. John uses the word thirty-six times in the book of 1 John. He introduces the letter with these phrases: "we have heard," "we have seen with our eyes," "our hands handled," and "by this we know that we have come to know Him. . . ." There is much we can know.

After reading Proverbs 8:17, "those who diligently seek me will find me," the prompt might lead one to write "I know from the experience of diligently seeking God in my prayer closet that he lives his life in and through me."

"I think" has a tentative quality. A person thinks about a reply but does not always know completely the proper response. Faith plays a larger role in the answer to this prompt.

When praying through the Gospel of Matthew, you will come to chapter 18:4: "Whoever then humbles himself as this child, he is the greatest in the kingdom of heaven." Your response might be, "Lord, I think about how much more maturity I must gain. Help me as I seek to humble myself before you."

"I wonder" allows your answer to soar to the heavens. There are no limits to this reaction prompt. Paul, in his first letter to the Corinthians 2:9, states: "Things which eye has not seen and ear has not heard, And which have not entered the heart of man, All that God has prepared for those who love Him." I wonder, you may write, what it is that God has prepared for me. Is it ———?

Contemporary Language

Sometimes we are prone to think that the Scriptures do not address us in the language of our time. Although I am not a party to that kind of thinking, I do find that I get quickly immersed in prayer by writing passages, especially the Psalms, in my own idiom. Psalm 100 begins:

> Shout joyfully to the LORD, all the earth.
> Serve the LORD with gladness;
> Come before Him with joyful singing.

In other words, look about you, trees, buildings, rivers, and every member of the human race. Give three cheers to the Lord. Put smiles on your faces. Praise all his doings here on earth. Get up, begin working, and sing a song full of the good news.

Some modern musical groups adopt the melodic idioms of the past. They perform the great musical classics, or move to the beat of Native American, Asian, or Hispanic cultures. Written prayer has the same possibilities for contemporary writers.

Letters to God

God has written to us; we can assume he would appreciate a response. Writing to God is as simple as writing a memo to a friend or co-worker. It might say something like the following:

Date: (Today)

Dear God,
  I was reading in your Book and had trouble under-
standing this statement: "Blessed are the meek." Did you
mean I should let people take advantage of me for their
personal gain, or something else? Also, I am having trou-
ble with my co-worker at the office. You know how he
teases me incessantly about my stand on alcohol. Show
me how to react to this pressure. I would appreciate an
answer soon, Lord, from your Word or however you wish
to speak to me. I wait patiently for your reply and trust
you for the answer.

Sincerely in your Son's name,
(Your name)

Perhaps you need to write a thank-you note:

Date: (Today)

Dear God,
  I want you to know how grateful I am for speaking to
me through your Word yesterday. My day went so well
after that.

With fondest regards,
(Your name)

A post-it note to God stuck on the refrigerator door is not in-
appropriate, either: "Lord, help me to stay out of here until
lunch time!"
  I discovered that answering a question as a letter or note
brings me into contact with Christ in a special way. Application K lists Jesus' questions found in the Gospels of Matthew,
Mark, Luke, and John. During my prayer time one morning I
answered him in the following manner:

John 6:67: "You do not want to go away also, do you?"
  No, Lord, of course not. I want to be as close to you as

I possibly can. But, Lord, you know my carnal nature. All
too often, I slip, regress, go back. I need the gentle, but
forceful, tugging of your Spirit to constantly keep me
in line.

Do I want to go away? No, Lord, a thousand times no. I
want to abide in you, be part of you.

Thank you, Lord.

Love,
Arnie

Double-Entry Notebook

Draw a line down the center of a blank sheet of paper. Place
the word *Entry* at the top of the left side. Here you will write
the exact words that you find in Scripture. On the top of the
right side write the word *Reaction.* The right side should include whatever comes to mind as you react to the Scripture
written on the left side. This reaction can take the form of a
poem, focused free-writing, a summary statement, a phrase,
an outline, a single word, a narrative, a letter, or any other appropriate response (see application H; see also Berthoff 1981,
45–46, for a discussion of the double-entry notebook).

Storying

Storying is a technique for creating a story from something
that has no plot. For instance, in Psalm 142, David is found in
a cave bewailing the plight of being pursued by his enemies.
He calls out to the Lord:

I cry aloud with my voice to the LORD;
I make supplication with my voice to the LORD.
I pour out my complaint before Him;
I declare my trouble before Him (Ps 142:1–2).

To "story" this psalm, go into the cave imaginatively. Feel
the loneliness and despair, sense the coldness of the walls.
Watch the flickering candlelight as you observe David putting

his thoughts into verse to God the Father. The following paragraphs are an example of storying:

> David shudders as the coldness of the cavern walls pene-
> trates his muscles and seeps into his bones. He turns to
> one of his men to talk, but each sleeps the sleep of the
> exhausted. So he takes his pen, and by the eerie glow of
> the candle, begins to write. As he concludes the poem,
> he hears a shout at the mouth of the cave. Immediately,
> all are awake and the candle is swiftly snuffed out. Every
> man is motionless except the silent movement of fingers
> wrapping around sword handles.
>
> A thought sweeps across David's mind from the
> last verse he just wrote, "For Thou wilt deal bountifully
> with me." May it be so, he whispers inwardly. Slowly, he
> crawls to the mouth of the cave.

Stream of Consciousness

Stream of consciousness is a technique of composition where
the writer, using first-person narration, tells the thoughts of a
particular person in a story. During the narrative, one learns
the psychological processes of that person at a pivotal point in
the story. If this technique intrigues you as a writer, try it with
various characters in Scripture who have strong personalities,
such as Moses, Joseph, Peter, Thomas, Stephen, or Paul.
Mentally go back in time and sit with the writer of a Scripture
passage (David, perhaps, writing the letter that will send Uriah
to his death). Write what you perceive is happening in David's
mind as a stream of consciousness while he writes the letter.

Present, Past, and Future Tenses

Choose a parable from the Scriptures (see application J). Shift
the narrative into a tense that is different from that of the
Scripture. Identify with an onlooker as you describe the situation from his or her point of view. If you choose the future
tense, it may be the present or years from now. Then, assume
the part of the other characters who are involved, that is, be-

come part of the event by identifying yourself with active participants in the scene. Dramatization is the key.

Five-Point Appraisal

Imposing a structure or type of classification on portions of Scripture can help a person develop understanding and gain additional insights. Using the Scriptures as a catalyst five categories can be used to glean meaning:

1. *Analyzing*
   Analyzing requires us to recognize and apply logic to the solution of a particular problem. *Analysis* means to examine methodically by separating the problem into parts, so we can detect the disposition of the problem as a whole. Using colored pens and pencils to highlight these relationships often helps.

2. *Inferring*
   Inferring means we study the information that we are given and draw a reasonable conclusion from the facts, as one would reason deductively.

3. *Predicting*
   When we predict, we project a conclusion based on the information given in a particular situation.

4. *Hypothesizing*
   To hypothesize, we use assumptions or premises to form a conclusion or an explanation that makes sense.

5. *Problem Solving*
   Problem solving involves finding creative ways to resolve a problem in a situation that presents uncertainty or perplexity.

There are many situations in the Scriptures that need creative solutions. One dilemma of Solomon's is a case in point. Two women came to Solomon, each declaring she was the same child's mother. When Solomon demanded, "Get me a sword. . . . Divide the living child in two, and give half to the one and half to the other," the real mother gave up her right so the child would be spared (1 Kgs 3:24–25).

In another case, Jesus had to gauge the will of the men standing before him. They brought to Jesus a woman accused of being caught in the act of adultery. He lingered over his decision while writing in the sand and finally said, "He who is without sin among you, let him be the first to throw a stone at her" (Jn 8:7).

How would you have addressed these difficult problems? You can ask yourself these questions when you come upon them in Scripture. The five-point appraisal, used with a verse from Scripture such as Psalm 5:3, provides some interesting insights:

> In the morning, O LORD, Thou wilt hear my voice;
> In the morning, I will order my prayer to Thee and
>   eagerly watch.

Analyzing—Logically, it makes sense to pray in the morning when I am fresh from a good night's sleep.

Inferring—It is reasonable to conclude that God will be up in the morning to hear my prayer, because "He who keeps you will not slumber" (Ps 121:3). So I can infer with certainty that he will be available to me.

Predicting—Based on the information given here, God will hear my voice when I order my prayer to him. I will now eagerly wait for his answer.

Hypothesizing—The assumptions (hypotheses) are that (1) God exists, (2) he hears in the morning, and (3) he hears my individual voice among all the others that call to him. Based on these hypotheses, which I believe to be true, I can bring an orderly prayer to him. Beyond that, I will eagerly watch for the answer to my prayer.

Problem Solving—My only dilemma in this entire exercise is, how in the world can God hear and act on so many voices at once? All I can say is that, because I have experienced solutions to my problems through prayer, he does respond.

Every category may not always yield appropriate meaning from Scripture. If this is the case, go to the next category and come back later.

Schemata

Schemata, the plural for *schema,* are cognitive arrangements designed to help one understand material that is difficult to comprehend. These groupings furnish structures for understanding new information. Further, they sometimes allow one to know what to anticipate from forthcoming data. (For a more complete explanation of schemata see Dembo 1988, 341–43.)

The sentence structure of some of Paul's writing in Ephesians and other epistles and letters appears convoluted and, often, hard to understand. Complicating the situation even further are the various translations that the writings have been through as well as Paul's unique way of thinking. Creating a schema, or mechanical layout, of the text permits one to see the textual material from another perspective. Schemata are a layman's approach to *hermeneutics,* which is, according to the dictionary, "the science and methodology of interpretation, especially of Scriptural text." (For additional insight on this process see McQuilkin 1992. His ideas form the background for this section).

One way of visually organizing a passage of text is to approach 1 John 2:7–8 with a schematic arrangement. The text reads:

> Beloved, I am not writing a new commandment to you, but an old commandment which you have had from the beginning; the old commandment is the word which you have heard. On the other hand, I am writing a new commandment to you, which is true in Him and in you, because the darkness is passing away, and the true light is already shining.

These verses, put into a schema, help one take a more intense, prayerful look at Scripture:

[7] Beloved
    I am not writing
        a new commandment
            to you,

but
>   [I am writing]
>   an old commandment
>   which you have had
>   from the beginning;
>   the old commandment is the word
>   which you have heard.
> ⁸ On the other hand,
>   I am writing
>   a new commandment
>   to you,
>   which is true

in Him
and
in you,

because

the darkness is passing away,
and
the true light is already shining.

Sentences often contain three elements:

1. Complete thoughts—independent or main clauses

2. Incomplete thoughts—dependent or subordinate clauses

3. Connecting words—prepositions and conjunctions

In verse 7 the complete, or independent, clause is "I am not writing a new commandment to you"; the incomplete, or dependent, clause is "an old commandment which you have had from the beginning"; the connecting word, or coordinating conjunction, is the word *but*. As one explores a passage in this manner, more insights are likely to surface and questions will arise that demand an answer. They will probably not be mind-blowing, but rather mind-searching. Start with a thought such as "I wonder what Paul really meant in verse 8 when he said, 'which is true *in* Him *and in* you'?"

The following should help you identify elements in a sentence as you form your schemata:

Connecting words include prepositions and conjunctions.

Prepositions link nouns and pronouns: Jesus walked *on* water. The preposition *on* links the word *water* to the verb *walked*.

Coordinating conjunctions such as *and, but, or, nor, for, so, yet,* join words, phrases, or clauses of equal grammatical rank: "in Him *and* in you." The conjunction *and* links the words *Him* and *you,* which is a nice thought when you pause to think about it.

Subordinating conjunctions join clauses that are not equal in rank: *"If I* just touch His garments, I shall get well"* (Mk 5:28). The dependent or subordinate clause, "If I just touch His garments" cannot stand by itself as a sentence; it must be joined to the independent or main clause, "I shall get well." And so another truth surfaces.

I believe writers need to periodically review, at least once a year, a standard grammatical text to sharpen their writing skills. I recommend the *Prentice-Hall Handbook for Writers* by Glenn Legett, C. David Mead, and Melinda G. Kramer (1991).

Interviewing Biblical Characters

As you pray, you may want to pray with the life of a favorite biblical character so that your own life may catch glimpses of his or her qualities. Then pray those characteristics or qualities into your own lifestyle.

Ask questions of your character. Do your homework. Find out what the person you are interviewing has done by checking facets of his or her background. The following list and series of questions should guide you. Search the Scriptures for the answers.

Mother/Father

Occupation

Age at the time of the interview

Education

Marriage and children

Next, ask the following questions of the biblical character and then try to answer them:

1. What person most influenced you in your youth or adult life?

2. What effect has that person had on you specifically?

3. What was the lowest point in your life? Why?

4. Do you believe people can change for the better? For the worse?

5. When did you last cry? What were the circumstances?

6. You (say, for example, Peter) are known as a rough, uncut diamond sort of person. How do you respond to that kind of characterization?

Then, ask the same questions, prayerfully, of yourself and pray-write the answers.

Answering Questions

Jesus was always asking questions—penetrating questions, such as, "Who is My mother and who are My brothers?" (Mt 12:48) and "Why are you asking me about what is good?" (Mt 19:17). Those questions, uttered two thousand years ago, still come into our lives, daring us to answer them without reservation.

In the four Gospels, more than three hundred questions are asked by Jesus, including "How many loaves do you have?" (Mt 15:34). A query like this requires a simple answer: "Seven, and a few small fish." Jesus also asked questions of an analytical and evaluative nature: "For which is easier, to say, 'Your sins are forgiven,' or to say, 'Rise, and walk'?" (Mt 9:5). In another example, the Jews took up stones against Christ when he declared, "I and the Father are one" (Jn 10:30). Jesus countered with, "I showed you many good works from the Father; for which of them are you stoning Me?" (Jn 10:32).

Jesus directed his questions at individuals or groups. Occasionally, he framed them within his parables, at other times the characters in his stories asked the questions. They still wait for our answers. As you pray through the Gospels, answer them in writing (see application K for a list with which to begin).

Search Paul's writing in the Scriptures for queries. He posed some fascinating questions that deserve our attention:

. . . . Is God the God of Jews only? Is He not the God of Gentiles also? (Rom 3:29).

. . . . Do you not know that all of us who have been baptized into Christ Jesus have been baptized into His death? (Rom 6:3).

Who shall separate us from the love of Christ? Shall tribulation, or distress, or persecution, or famine, or nakedness, or peril, or sword? (Rom 8:35).

O death, where is your victory? O death, where is your sting? (1 Cor 15:55).

This is the only thing I want to find out from you: did you receive the Spirit by the works of the Law, or by hearing with faith? (Gal 3:2).

Where then is that sense of blessing you had? (Gal 4:15).

You were running well; who hindered you from obeying the truth? (Gal 5:7).

The most challenging questions in the Bible are found in the Book of Job, especially in Job 38 and 39. These queries could keep one occupied for many years, perhaps even a lifetime. There "the Lord answered Job out of the whirlwind. . . ."

Where were you when I laid the foundation of the earth!
Tell Me, if you have understanding,
Who set its measurements, since you know?

Or who stretched the line on it?
On what were its bases sunk?
Or who laid its cornerstone,
When the morning stars sang together,
And all the sons of God shouted for joy? (Jb 38:4–7).

Job, like us, can only conclude: "Behold, I am insignificant; what can I reply to Thee? I lay my hand on my mouth" (Jb 40:4).

The afflicted shall eat and
be satisfied;
Those who seek Him will
praise the LORD.
Let your heart live forever!

Psalm 22:26

4

Amplifying on a Theme

Writing—A Way to Pray deals with *imaging*. This is not a word to shy away from, for the Scriptures declare its importance by using the word *image* five times in the Book of Genesis:

> Then God said, "Let Us make man in Our image, according to Our likeness . . ." (Gn 1:26).

> And God created man in His own image, in the image of God He created him; male and female He created them (Gn 1:27).

> When Adam had lived one hundred and thirty years, he became the father of a son in his own likeness, according to his image, and named him Seth (Gn 5:3).

> Whoever sheds man's blood, By man his blood shall be shed, For in the image of God He made man (Gn 9:6).

Because humankind has applied and exercised its imagination, spectacular advances have been made in the arts, literature, industry, and sciences. Capturing the imagination in a simple definition is difficult, if at all possible. Perhaps it is better to describe the function of the imagination as Janet Emig does:

> The imagination: What is it? The mind actively constructing the not-here; the not-now; the not-me. The mind actively constructing actual worlds inhabited by actual others, others who breathe and bleed, think and feel. The mind constructing possible worlds inhabited by possible others. The mind constructing and furnishing the interior of one's own sensibility (1983, 177).

Richard Foster examines images in a section on sanctifying the imagination in his book *Prayer: Finding the Heart's True Home:* "The simplest and most basic way to meditate upon the text of Scripture is through the imagination. . . . We must not despise this simpler, more humble route into God's presence. Jesus himself taught in this manner, making constant appeal to the imagination in his parables" (1992, 147).

Chapter 4 contains writing techniques that figure prominently in processing the imagination. Consider a word of caution, though, before entering this area—what one imagines is not necessarily God-breathed or inspired by the Holy Spirit. Similarly, an inspired thought is not necessarily from God. To assume that a momentary inspiration is part of God's perfect plan of action is to court disaster. One must distinguish between the voice of God and the voice of one's muse. When in doubt, trust the Scriptures as they uncover truth in totality, not in specificity. Put your inspiration on the back burner of accountability. You would not, I hope, send off a manuscript that was hastily written over the weekend to a publisher on Monday. It takes care; it takes time.

Fictionalizing Events

Many actual events in Scripture are just waiting for an imaginative entrance into your prayer periods. The parables, remember, are fiction; they are stories created to send a spiritual message to listeners. As you create fictionalized events, keep in mind that poetic license allows their development to occur. As you meditate on incidents, new insights will emerge. You will develop a closeness with the message and the messenger that cannot be experienced with casual reading of the narrative.

For example, I was praying through Matthew 8:1–5. In my prayer writing, I fictionalized the passage. The following story became prayer—my conscious relationship with the Father:

> Jesus picked his way among the rocks as he came down from the mountainside. Men, women, and children followed him, jumping, calling to one another. Parents shouted to their children to stay close by. "Joshua, behave. Take your sister by the hand." "Samuel, watch your little brother. Keep together. Keep up. We'll meet at the foot of the mountain. Don't get lost!"
>
> Jesus smiled as he listened to the families following him. Some ran ahead. Some ran beside him. Little children clasped his hand vying for his attention. The day was glorious.
>
> Suddenly a numbing hush washed over the multitude, bringing them to an instant standstill. From behind an embankment at the foot of the mountain stood a man. The grotesqueness of his features made many pull their tunics close about themselves. Silence hung as a wet cloth clinging to a rock.
>
> The leper bowed down before Christ, saying, "Lord, if You are willing, You can make me clean."
>
> Jesus, in the quietness of the moment, held out his hand, touched the leprous man and pronounced, "I am willing. Be cleansed."
>
> The man's disfigurement disappeared before the crowd's eyes. No one, not even the children, dared move. They stood transfixed.
>
> Jesus broke the silence by saying quietly, "See that you tell no one; but go, show yourself to the priest, and present the offering that Moses commanded, for a testimony to them."

By fictionalizing this event as a prayer, I more fully experienced the episode as an "I am there" encounter.

Here is what one might do with the account of the disciples as they discussed who among them was the greatest. The first

verse of the narrative in Mark 9:33 begins with these words:
"And they came to Capernaum; and when He was in the
house, He began to question them, 'What were you dis-
cussing on the way?'"

If you chose Peter for the viewpoint character, he might
begin in this fashion:

> My name is Peter, one of the twelve disciples. One of my
> most embarrassing moments, and that of the disciples,
> began on a typical day for that time of year. The lake
> area was cooled by an eastern breeze. We received an
> invitation to someone's home. Whose home it was, I am
> not sure. Unexpectedly, the Master asked us about the
> discussion we were having along the way. We looked at
> each other in amazement. How could he know?

After one prays-writes such an event, it is easier to comprehend the point of the lesson or to sense its impact.

The following is another Scripture passage from which I
gained insight as I prayed-wrote it. The event is in Matthew
9:14–15.

> John the Baptist's followers came to Jesus.
> "Look," they said, "we fast. The Pharisees fast. But do
> Your disciples fast? No. They don't. The question is both-
> ering us and we want to know why."
> Jesus became pensive for a moment before beginning
> his response. Then he looked up and said, "Think of it
> this way. A bridegroom is about to be married. He has
> his friends around him, probably for the last time as a
> group. Are they going to mourn now because they will
> not have him much longer in their fellowship? Of course
> not. They are going to rejoice with him in the present.
> They will eat with him, enjoy him. Make every minute
> with him count. Ah, but when the bridegroom is gone,
> taken away, then they will mourn and fast. That will be
> the appropriate time for them to do so."

Read a passage, such as a parable in the Gospels, and pray-
write it as if you are there, viewing the incident. You may want
to pray-write the scene as a character in the episode.

Clustering

Clustering is a word association technique. Gabriele Rico defines it in this way:

> Clustering is a nonlinear brainstorming process akin to free association. It makes an invisible Design-mind process visible through a nonlinear spilling out of lightning associations that allows patterns to emerge. Through clustering we naturally come up with a multitude of choices from a part of our mind where the experiences of a lifetime mill and mingle. It is the writing tool that accepts wondering, not-knowing, seeming chaos, gradually mapping an interior landscape as ideas begin to emerge. It is an openness to the unknown, an attitude that says "I wonder where this is taking me?" Clustering acknowledges that it's okay to start writing not knowing exactly what, where, who, when, and how. Most writers acknowledge that this is how it inevitably is anyway (1983, 28–29).

To apply the technique of clustering to prayer, take a theme from Scripture, such as benevolence, conscience, doubt, family, or love, and use it as a nucleus word. You may want to first read Scripture passages about your theme—or nucleus word—as referenced in a topical chain-reference Bible. Write this theme word in the upper third of a blank page. Then write whatever comes into your mind, in words or phrases, around your theme word. Let the words "cluster" around your original word until no other words are forthcoming. Circle words that cluster together and connect them by lines and arrows. When you have a sudden urge to write, begin. Rico says a shift in feeling may make one exclaim, "Aha! I think I know what I want to say" (ibid., 37).

As an example, if the theme word is *love,* you might begin with a cluster that resembles the following:

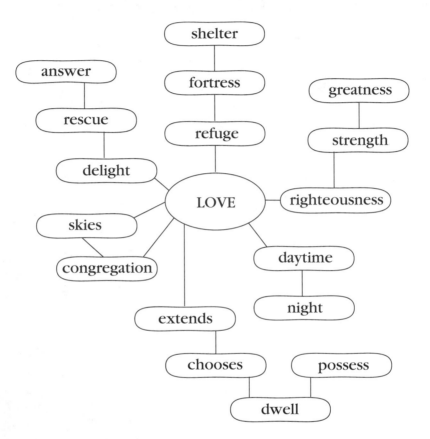

All of the words encircling the word *love* are from various passages throughout Scripture that refer to this theme. As you write, your prayer writing could become a paean of praise, a poem, or one of many prayer writing forms (see application L).

Another way to cluster is to follow the outline below:

1. Read a selection from Scripture.

2. Select a word from that portion of Scripture that intrigues you.

3. Write the word in the upper third of a blank page.

4. Around your original word, write words or phrases that you associate with its meaning.

5. After you have written ten or more associations, circle and connect those associations that have commonality. Continue writing words and connect them until you have exhausted your options and you feel compelled to begin your pray-write time.

6. Begin free-writing from the information in your cluster. This writing then becomes a continuation of your prayer.

After you pray-write your cluster into a format, survey what you have written and underline in colored pen the truths and insights that speak directly to you.

Script Writing

Scripts take various forms in our media-dominated culture: television, radio, motion pictures, stage plays, and reader's theater. Scripts have a format structurally different from other types of writing. A script written for a radio program might look like the one in application N.

When you pray-write by creating a script, you imagine yourself into a scene. The scriptural facts become your temporary reality. You sense an anticipation for the event that you do not experience through reading alone. You can practice running scenes back and forth in your mind as if you were a human VCR. Flick the rewind and fast-forward mechanisms and stop at any point to digest, scrutinize, and change your mental script. Look and listen into this scene in Matthew 9:9:

And as Jesus passed on from there, He saw a man, called Matthew, sitting in the tax office; and He said to him, "Follow Me!" And he rose, and followed Him.

He Saw a Man
[Jesus walks confidently, quietly, purposefully through the city. The sights and sounds of midday chatter

*envelop him. The dust of the streets makes low clouds
around his ankles. Turning to his right, Jesus looks
upon a tax collector. Jesus stops, catches his eye and
motions to him—]*

JESUS: Follow me!

*[Matthew walks confidently, quietly, purposefully
through the city—following Jesus. He saw a man.]*

This scene is short, therefore, easy to visualize and run
back and forth in one's mind, savoring each moment and
each spoken word. Try it.

Matthew 8:14–15 is also short, but allows for vividness of
sensory expression:

And when Jesus had come to Peter's home, He saw his
mother-in-law lying sick in bed with a fever. And He
touched her hand, and the fever left her; and she arose,
and waited on Him.

The Mother-in-Law
*[A sparsely furnished room in a small home in Palestine.
Light streams through an open window in a back bed-
room. In the shadows on a cot an old woman turns laboriously onto her side. A cloth covering the doorway
silently parts and Christ enters. The woman moans.]*

JESUS: (softly) Sister? You are not well?

[The elderly woman wipes her brow with a tattered cloth.]

WOMAN: Lord, do not enter. I am ill with fever. I do not
want you to catch what I have. I will be fine by tomorrow.

*[Jesus smiles and pulls a chair by her bed. He sits beside
her and places his hand on her forehead.]*

JESUS: Today you will prepare the meal for us.

[The woman sighs uncontrollably.]

Jesus: In the name of my Father, blessed mother-in-law of Peter, you are healed of your fever.

[The old woman stretches her limbs, pulls back the coverlet, folds her tattered cloth, and stands as Jesus straightens from his chair.]

Woman: My fever is gone! I feel fine now!

[Jesus smiles and guides her to the kitchen. Within moments she dismisses the help. One can hear her saying that she will prepare the meal, and only she, for the Master has said she would. Her son-in-law, Peter, leans against a wall smiling.]

Praying in this fashion uses images in a spectacular way. Habakkuk, perhaps, understood this possibility centuries before anyone ever thought of sending images electronically:

Then the Lord answered me and said,
"Record the vision
And inscribe it on tablets,
That the one who reads it may run.
For the vision is yet for the appointed time;
It hastens toward the goal, and it will not fail.
Though it tarries, wait for it;
For it will certainly come, it will not delay" (Hb 2:2–3).

Poetic Writing

Is poetic writing poetry? Probably not. In the writer's marketplace, writing becomes poetry when an editor writes: "Thank you for your submission. We will publish your poem in our magazine." Until that happens, what you and I write is poetic and nothing more.

Democritus (ca.460–ca.370 B.C.) wrote: "Whatever a poet writes with enthusiasm and a divine inspiration is very fine," (Bartlett 1968, 88). This sounds a bit like a teacher who does not want to discourage an aspiring poet, doesn't it? Perhaps we should leave the defining to someone else and appropriate William Stafford's definition: "A poem is anything said in such a way or put on a page in a such a way as to invite from the hearer or reader a certain kind of attention" (1987, 61). The Scriptures are brimming with poems, and much of the prose is decidedly poetic in rhythm and beat.

Neither poetry as a skill nor writing poetry as an occupation is of great import in Scripture. One exception in the Christian Scriptures is Paul's speech, possibly at the Council of the Areopagus, to the men of Athens. Paul quotes their own poets as saying "For we also are His [God's] offspring" (Acts 17:28).

The word *poet* in Greek *(poietes)* means a maker or a doer. This definition of a poet as having a positive or forceful demeanor is not generally familiar to us. Similarly, people who pray are not considered makers and doers. However, poets are the movers and shakers of the world, as are prayer warriors. Rulers and dictators throughout the centuries found it necessary to jail, persecute, and murder poets and practicing Christians to retain their power base.

The Scriptures, both Hebrew and Christian, are full of poetry of various kinds. Read again, slowly, the Magnificat:

And Mary said:
"My soul exalts the Lord,
And my spirit has rejoiced in God my Savior.
For He has had regard for the humble state of His
    bondslave;
For behold, from this time on all generations will
    count me blessed.
For the Mighty One has done great things for me;
And holy is His name.
And His mercy is upon generation after generation
Toward those who fear Him.
He has done mighty deeds with His arm;
He has scattered those who were proud in the thoughts
    of their heart.
He has brought down rulers from their thrones,
And has exalted those who were humble.
He has filled the hungry with good things;
And sent away the rich empty-handed.
He has given help to Israel His servant,

In remembrance of His mercy,
As He spoke to our fathers,
To Abraham and his offspring forever" (Lk 1:46–55).

Two kinds of parallelisms in the Proverbs make you stop and think. In *synonymous parallelisms*, a reiteration of a basic truth uses different words in each line. The following passages are examples of synonymous parallelisms:

Let your eyes look directly ahead,
And let your gaze be straight in front of you (Prv 4:25).

The fear of the LORD is the beginning of wisdom,
And the knowledge of the Holy One is understanding (Prv 9:10).

In *antithetic parallelisms,* one viewpoint is in the first line and a dissimilar one in the second. The following are examples of antithetic parallelisms:

He who goes about as a talebearer reveals secrets,
But he who is trustworthy conceals a matter (Prv 11:13).

A gentle answer turns away wrath,
But a harsh word stirs up anger (Prv 15:1).

Pray-write parallelisms from the Proverbs into your own words as part of your prayer experience.

Often, as one reads Scripture slowly, paragraphs seem to echo themselves in interesting patterns, much like the parallelisms just discussed. When you come upon these, you may want to rewrite them in poetic ways to discover new meanings. Culling from verses in Ephesians 4:17–20 and 28–32, I created this poetic form that brought forth some new insights to me:

Walking
    in the futility of mind
        darkened in understanding

          excluded from God
          hardened of heart
          calloused
          practicing impurity
   a walk not learned in Christ
Performing
     with your hands
        sharing in needs
        proceeding in edification
        sealed in redemption
        tender-hearted
        practicing forgiveness
   a performance learned in Christ

We can also look to the Psalms as poems of great and ever-lasting beauty. The writer at prayer has tremendous opportunities for using the Psalms as a catalyst for poetic writing. I pray-write poetic writing extensively from the Psalms, though the genre is not my forte. The poetic musing, forever sealed in a blank-paged hardbound book, will never see the light of an editor's lamp. From time to time I read my poetic writings and rejoice in the insights and joy they gave me when I first wrote them. I also realize why they must remain hidden from the view of the public, as one would a personal diary or journal. I will share a few to display my own lack of a gift in this area as an act of encouragement to others. May the faint of heart among you use this method to develop a closer relationship with the Father.

Luke 20:26 impressed me during my prayer time some months ago. It reads: "And they were unable to catch Him in a saying in the presence of the people; and marveling at His answer, they became silent." This eventually became the following poetic writing:

Interlude
Their incessant chatter,
born of lies,
desirous beyond reason to capture him,
began its quick decline
into silence,

> · and he became the One
>   whom all men do
>   obeisance,
>   for within him
>   was the Father.

Using lingering writing, focused free-writing, the double-entry notebook, stream of consciousness, or clustering with the catalyst of the Psalms or other Scriptures may generate praying-writing of a poetic nature in your journal too.

This brings us to the simplest of poetic writing: the two-word poem. The two-word poem is exactly that, two words as a line, strung out in a vertical column. Children love to do them because, in essence, they are playing with language. So be a child for a moment. See how a simple act of language elicits absorbing insights.

While we do not know exactly how Jesus spoke, in terms of sentence length, one could imply from the translations that he was economical in his speech. Jesus' commands were terse: "Follow Me," "Daughter, take courage," "Stretch out your hand," "Begone Satan!" Those who gave us chapter and verse markings for our present Bibles several centuries ago felt compelled to accent two words that many a child has fallen back on when asked to recite a Scripture memory verse: "Jesus wept" (Jn 11:35).

The following is an example of a two-word poem from Psalm 60:11–12:

> Give help
> Against adversary
> Man's deliverance
> Is vain
> Through God
> Do valiantly
> He will
> Tread down
> Our adversaries

Three-word poems are simple to construct and writing them often allows you to search the mind of God and enjoy his presence. Your poems may not make sense to others;

however, if they breathe the presence of God into your life, be thankful. The following poem is from Deuteronomy 6:4–9:

God is One!
you shall love
   all your heart
   all your soul
   all your might
you shall teach
you shall talk
   in your house
   when you walk
   when you rest
you shall bind
   on your hand
   on your forehead
you shall write
   on the doorpost
   on your gates

If you wish, you can combine two- and three-word poem forms, like this one from Isaiah 9:6:

Prince of Peace
child born us
son given us
government will rest
on His shoulders
His name called
   Wonderful Counselor
   Mighty God
   Eternal Father
   Peace Prince

You can also rearrange your page, as in this poetic writing from Matthew 11:28–30:

Come to Me
   all who weary
      I give rest

take My yoke
 learn from Me
  I am gentle
   humble in heart
    you find rest
     for your souls
      My yoke easy
       My yoke light

Playing with language is similar to enjoying God. We distance ourselves from the Creator because of the description of him in the Hebrew Scriptures. We find difficulty in intimate abiding. We sing "and he walks with me and he talks with me," but discover that we do not experience him as reality in our every day, minute-by-minute experience. By praying two- and three-word poems while waiting for a bus or a spouse, we can intuit a God who is enjoyable to be around. More important, he may find us enjoyable to be with! (For an engaging book that challenges the portrait of a faraway God, see Trueblood 1964.) God is as close to us as the spoken word. He lives in our language. "But thou art holy, O thou that inhabitest the praises of Israel" (Ps 22:3, King James Bible).

Your poetic writing may be free or blank verse, rhymed or unrhymed, or structured as the classical Japanese haiku—three lines of five, seven, and five syllables, unrhymed with a hint of a season. Then you may wish to try one of the haiku derivatives such as the tanka, renga, and senryu. For a number of poetic writing patterns, see my book *The Poetry Corner.*

The following is a haiku, with its syllabic breakdown, from Psalm 30:5:

(5) weeping in the night
(7) dawn now breaks, warm joy surges
(5) his favor arrives

The *cinquain,* an American creation by Adelaide Crapsey (1878–1914), comes from the French word *cinq,* meaning five. It is five lines in length with specific internal features, and a syllabic structure for each line of two, four, six, eight, and two.

The following is a syllabic cinquain from Psalm 31:

(2) Title	O Lord!
(4) Description of title	God of all truth
(6) Action	Deliver and guide me
(8) Feeling	I cry for strength, for courage now
(2) Another word for the title	My King!

Ottone M. Riccio, in his chapter on the brain and heart in *The Intimate Art of Writing Poetry,* has a section titled "Thematic Sources Outside the Self," which is pertinent to this discussion because scriptural themes in *Writing—A Way to Pray* are proposed as sources for writers to use as catalysts for prayer:

> All around you exist thousands of reasons for poems: people with whom you come in contact or read or hear about; events you witness; relationships you observe: the child and parent, playmates, siblings, adults at war, adults in love; the phenomena of the natural environment; the industrial, militaristic, socialistic, or whatever society you view, ponder, interpret, report on; the past, future, or present. As a writer you have the obligation to listen, watch, take notes (mentally at least), evaluate, and understand in the context of an event's happening (1980, 24).

As you read the Psalms, especially those penned by David, and use them as prayer, visualize David praying-writing about his relationships and conflicts. There is much to pray-write about. Poetic writing is another way to express your consciousness of God.

You may want to write something poetic based on a character in the Word. Peter is one of my favorites, for, like me, he needed a second chance, and he took it and did well.

Second Chance
"Who," the Lord said,
"say ye that I am?"

And Peter of the First Chance
    said, "You are the Christ,
the Son of the living God."
"Come," the Lord said,
    and Peter walked on water

And then there was Peter
Who sank into the deep
Who fell asleep
    and could not spend one hour
Who cursed his Lord
    disowned him

But Jesus
    sent a message
    from beyond the grave
"Go and tell my disciples
    and Peter"

And so began
    Peter of the Second Chance.

My prayer for you as a writer is that you will take advantage of the second chance and turn the prayer key now placed in your hands. Come! Catch glimpses of truth through the pray-write experience.

Open my eyes that I may see
Glimpses of truth thou hast for me;
Place in my hands the wonderful key
That shall unclasp, and set me free:

Silently now I wait for thee,
Ready, my God, thy will to see;
Open my eyes, illumine me, Spirit divine!

(Words by Clara H. Scott, Baptist hymnal, 1875.)

Application A

An Approach to Prayer

Praying is as much an ongoing process of spiritual development as writing is a process of intellectual development. Stagnant prayer requires the nourishment of practice. At this time I still find God mostly through the experience of prayer writing. Perhaps that will change too. If so, it will be into a realm of prayer that will be more conducive to my understanding of the mystery of God and the worship of him.

Let me describe to you how I am operating now. I tell you this not as a goal for you to pursue, but because, in my experience, the people I know and trust as Christian believers, many of whom are pastors, seldom open this secret compartment of their spiritual lives. Jesus did when he stated, "Pray, then, in this way" (Mt 6:9).

I arise in the morning, generally between five and six o'clock, the time when I am most spiritually and mentally alert. Often, I take a moment to sit on the edge of my bed and thank God for the night of rest and the knowledge he has revealed to me (cf. Ps 19:2). Then I go to my "inner room" (Mt. 6:6), which for me is the loft on the second floor of our home. There I get comfortable in a hard-backed chair and open my Bible to the Psalms. I have nearby a dictionary, an exhaustive Hebrew and Greek concordance, and a notebook. I open my notebook to the blank page after the last entry and write down the date, time, and day. Sitting quietly, I relax prayerfully, allowing God's presence to enter my life. As I do this I confess my sin and tell him of my need for the energizing will of his life in mine. This purging is extremely important in my view. I ask Christ to sit with me, suggesting he sit beside me in the chair I keep especially for him.

-•

Psalm Prayer

My first entry in the notebook is the psalm with which I choose to begin my prayer time. Verse by verse, I slowly write the psalm exactly as it is found in the Scriptures. The writing might appear in a double-entry notebook format or may assume a schemata approach. After jotting down the Scripture, I react to it in focused free-writing. Colored pens help me to analyze my interpretation and connect it to the original writing. A psalm prayer may last fifteen to thirty minutes and often as long as one hour.

The Psalms infuse new meaning into my life each time I read them. Having written them dozens of times, I find that the message I receive synergistically explodes into my consciousness with renewed understanding and hope. For example, in the passage where David calls down the wrath and retribution of God on his enemies, I understand David's anguish at the hounding of his foes. I sense, then, that I too can be distraught and tell God my innermost feelings without fear of reprisal. God does not hold me accountable for being human; he created me that way. He does, however, hold me accountable for what I do and say.

Scriptural Prayer

The second portion of my prayer time is spent in scriptural prayer. At this juncture, I pray-write primarily from the Epistles or Proverbs. I often underline with colored pens those aspects of Scripture that speak to me about what I should ask the Father, things of personal benefit or for the benefit of others. James admonishes us, "You ask and do not receive, because you ask with wrong motives, so that you may spend it on your pleasures" (Jas 4:3). I have found that praying the Scriptures gives me a better opportunity to ask for things that God wants to give to me rather than making up a list of my personal desires, which are all too often fraught with wrong motives. Again, I write out a verse or several verses prayerfully and react to them in writing as suggested previously. I also use this time to answer the same questions that Jesus asked of those who listened to him (see application K). Many of these questions lead me into areas that I would not have considered otherwise.

Gospel Prayer

I spend the third portion of my prayer time in the Gospels of Matthew, Mark, Luke, and John. Often, for several weeks at a time, I write just the words of Christ and react to them. At other times, especially in Mark's Gospel, I read one of his action-packed stories and write it as if I were there. I react to the story as Jesus, one of his apostles, or an adult or child sitting in the background might view the scene. Sometimes the prayer becomes a script (see application N). When I am praying the Sermon on the Mount, I spend time with a specific Beatitude and write out its personal meaning. After I am finished, as I listen to Christ speak to me through the Gospels, I sometimes find that I can grasp his message more completely by praying through poetic writing on the passage I am reading. God also speaks to me through poetic writing when I am in the Psalms.

Topical Prayer

The fourth element in my prayer relationship with the Lord is meditating on a topic or theme. My topical chain-reference Bible lists various themes that run throughout the Scriptures: atonement, Christ, faith, justification, love, patience, repentance, righteousness, self-denial, truth, wisdom, worship, and many more. Most of these themes, if not all, begin in Genesis. I follow them through the Hebrew and Christian Scriptures, writing and reacting to them as I trace their pathway. This allows me to touch the whole of the Word of God during each prayer session.

When meditating on a specific theme, I often draw truth from previous prayer sessions of my pray-write time. It is as if the Lord says, "See, I explained that to you before, Arnold. Now, doesn't it make more sense to you?" I write, "Yes, Lord. Thank you."

Promises Prayer

The fifth allotment of my morning prayer time is my reaction to the prayer promises in application B. I reread them, write what they mean to me that particular day, and open my mind to new meanings as to how the Hebrew Scriptures relate to the Christian Scriptures.

The prayer promises are organized in such a way that I can read one verse from the Hebrew Scriptures and one from the Christian Scriptures every day of the month. Boredom is not likely, but if for some reason bordom does set in, search the Scriptures—there are literally hundreds more from which to choose. Read what Herbert Lockyer says about the study of the promises contained in the Scriptures:

> The fact that all God's promises are stated in clear, simple terminology adds to their value. They are not expressed in ambiguous terms, but with the greatest clarity and perspicuity. It is not His will to leave His people in uncertainty concerning His kind and gracious intentions toward them. The divine promises are never wordy, nor are they couched in complex, mystifying language for "God is light, and in Him is no darkness at all" (1 Jn 1:5). All He has to say is set forth in clear, intelligible words, so that even the wayfarer cannot err therein. If the full meaning of a promise appears doubtful in one place it is abundantly cleared up in other promises.
>
> Neither are the promises expressed in any cold or reserved manner. Because he wanted no dullness or slowness to believe all that he has promised, God condescended to make use of the strongest, simplest words and phrases language could furnish. Thus we have a great variety of choice expressions to convince us of the assurances of His favor (1962, 16).

When I am finished writing, I close with "I love you," and write my name.

Intercessory Prayer

The last portion of my prayer time is intercessory. Here I pray over a list that includes names of friends, relatives, missionaries, and people from my church who are in need (see application C). I also pray over a special sheet that lists deeply personal needs of my own, along with the needs of close friends. This special sheet begins with an admonition to pray about specific items for that day. I pray about such mundane things as my breakfast, my exercise program, and the people and places I will be involved with that day or later in the week. I close by meditating or singing from a sheet of hymns or choruses—"singing and making melody with your heart to the Lord" as suggested by Paul (Eph 5:19).

This is my prayer pattern at the present time. It does not include my evening prayer periods, fasting and prayer times, prayer for those brought to my attention by the reading of the newspaper or the watching of television newscasts, or non-imaging means of entering into the presence of the Father.

Each of you must find your own way. Ann and Barry Ulanov say it very well: "There is no right way to pray. The more we pray and the more we learn about the way others pray, the more sure we become about this. Different approaches abound to provide room for each of us to explore, improvise, and find his or her own way in prayer" (1982, 115).

And so it should be.

Application B

Prayer Promises

Verses from the Hebrew and Christian Scriptures for Each Day of the Month

Day 1

Jos 1:8

This book of the law shall not depart from your mouth, but you shall meditate on it day and night, so that you may be careful to do according to all that is written in it; for then you will make your way prosperous, and then you will have success.

2 Pt 1:4

For by these He has granted to us His precious and magnificent promises, in order that by them you might become partakers of the divine nature, having escaped the corruption that is in the world by lust.

Day 2

2 Chr 7:14

. . . and [if] My people who are called by My name humble themselves and pray, and seek My face and turn from their wicked ways, then I will hear from heaven, will forgive their sin, and will heal their land.

Jn 15:7

If you abide in Me, and My words abide in you, ask whatever you wish, and it shall be done for you.

Day 3

Jer 33:3

Call to Me, and I will answer you, and I will tell you great and mighty things, which you do not know.

Jn 14:13–14

And whatever you ask in My name, that I will do, that the Father may be glorified in the Son. If you ask Me anything in My name, I will do it.

Day 4
Is 40:31
Yet those who wait for the
LORD
Will gain new strength;
They will mount up with
wings like eagles,
They will run and not get
tired,
They will walk and not be-
come weary.

Mt 11:28–29
Come to Me, all who are
weary and heavy-laden, and
I will give you rest. Take My
yoke upon you, and learn
from Me, for I am gentle
and humble in heart; and
you shall find rest for your
souls.

Day 5
Prv 3:5–6
Trust in the LORD with all
your heart,
And do not lean on your
own understanding.
In all your ways acknowl-
edge Him,
And He will make your
paths straight.

1 Jn 2:25
And this is the promise
which He Himself made to
us: eternal life.

Day 6
Ps 55:22
Cast your burden upon the
LORD, and He will sustain
you;
He will never allow the
righteous to be shaken.

1 Pt 5:7
. . . casting all your anxiety
upon Him, because He
cares for you.

Day 7
Is 41:10
Do not fear, for I am with
you;
Do not anxiously look about
you, for I am your God.
I will strengthen you, surely
I will help you,
Surely I will uphold you with
My righteous right hand.

Jn 14:18–19
I will not leave you as or-
phans; I will come to you.
After a little while the world
will behold Me no more;
but you will behold Me;
because I live, you shall live
also.

Day 8

Prv 8:17
I love those who love me;
And those who diligently
   seek me will find me.

Mt 5:6
Blessed are those who
hunger and thirst for righteousness, for they shall be
satisfied.

Day 9

Nm 23:19
God is not a man, that He
   should lie,
Nor a son of man, that He
   should repent;
Has He said, and will He
   not do it?
Or has He spoken, and will
   He not make it good?

Mt 18:19–20
Again I say to you, that if
two of you agree on earth
about anything that they
may ask, it shall be done for
them by My Father who is
in heaven. For where two or
three have gathered
together in My name, there I
am in their midst.

Day 10

Jos 23:14
. . . not one word of all the
good words which the Lord
your God spoke concerning
you has failed; all have been
fulfilled for you, not one of
them has failed.

Phil 4:6–7
Be anxious for nothing, but
in everything by prayer and
supplication with thanksgiving let your requests be
made known to God. And
the peace of God, which
surpasses all comprehen-
sion, shall guard your hearts
and your minds in Christ
Jesus.

Day 11

Ps 37:4–5
Delight yourself in the Lord;
And He will give you the
   desires of your heart.
Commit your way to the
   Lord,
Trust also in Him, and He
   will do it.

Phil 4:13
I can do all things through
Him who strengthens me.

Day 12

Is 26:3

The steadfast of mind Thou
    wilt keep in perfect peace,
Because he trusts in Thee.

Mt 6:34

Therefore do not be anxious
for tomorrow; for tomorrow
will care for itself. Each day
has enough trouble of its
own.

Day 13

Is 43:1

Do not fear, for I have redeemed you; I have called
you by name; you are Mine!

Eph 1:13

In Him, you also, after listening to the message of
truth, the gospel of your
salvation—having also be-
lieved, you were sealed in
Him with the Holy Spirit of
promise.

Day 14

Ps 126:5–6

Those who sow in tears
    shall reap with joyful
    shouting.
He who goes to and fro
    weeping, carrying his bag
    of seed,
Shall indeed come again
    with a shout of joy, bring-
    ing his sheaves with him.

Gal 6:7–8

Do not be deceived, God is
not mocked; for whatever a
man sows, this he will also
reap. For the one who sows
to his own flesh shall from
the flesh reap corruption,
but the one who sows to
the Spirit shall from the
Spirit reap eternal life.

Day 15

Is 55:11

So shall My word be which
goes forth from My
mouth;
It shall not return to Me
empty,
Without accomplishing what
I desire,
And without succeeding in
the matter for which I
sent it.

Jn 16:23–24

Truly, truly, I say to you, if
you shall ask the Father for
anything, He will give it to
you in My name. Until now
you have asked for nothing
in My name; ask, and you
will receive, that your joy
may be made full.

Day 16

Lam 3:22–23

The LORD's lovingkindnesses
indeed never cease,
For His compassions never
fail.
They are new every morn-
ing;
Great is Thy faithfulness.

1 Cor 10:13

No temptation has overtaken
you but such as is common
to man; and God is faithful,
who will not allow you to
be tempted beyond what
you are able, but with the
temptation will provide the
way of escape also, that you
may be able to endure it.

Day 17

Is 65:24

It will also come to pass that
before they call, I will answer; and while they are
still speaking, I will hear.

Mt 6:6

But you, when you pray, go
into your inner room, and
when you have shut your
door, pray to your Father
who is in secret, and your
Father who sees in secret
will repay you.

Day 18

Ps 34:8–9

O taste and see that the
   Lord is good;
How blessed is the man
   who takes refuge in Him!
O fear the Lord, you His
   saints;
For to those who fear Him,
   there is no want.

Jas 1:5

But if any of you lacks wisdom, let him ask of God, who gives to all men generously and without reproach, and it will be given to him.

Day 19

Mal 4:2

But for you who fear My name the sun of righteousness will rise with healing in its wings; and you will go forth and skip like calves from the stall.

Phil 1:6

For I am confident of this very thing, that He who began a good work in you will perfect it until the day of Christ Jesus.

Day 20

Is 33:15–16

He who walks righteously,
   and speaks with sincerity,
He who rejects unjust gain,
And shakes his hands so
   that they hold no bribe;
He who stops his ears from
   hearing about bloodshed,
And shuts his eyes from
   looking upon evil;
He will dwell on the
   heights;
His refuge will be the impregnable rock;
His bread will be given him;
His water will be sure.

Heb 4:16

Let us therefore draw near with confidence to the throne of grace, that we may receive mercy and may find grace to help in time of need.

Day 21

Is 1:18
"Come now, and let us rea-
son together,"
Says the LORD,
"Though your sins are as
scarlet,
They will be as white as
snow;
Though they are red like
crimson,
They will be like wool."

Mk 10:26–27
And they were more aston-
ished and said to Him,
"Then who can be saved?"
Looking upon them, Jesus
said, "With men it is impossible, but not with God; for
all things are possible with
God."

Day 22

Is 43:25
I, even I, am the one who
wipes out your transgres-
sions for My own sake;
And I will not remember
your sins.

Gal 3:26
For you are all sons of God
through faith in Christ Jesus.

Day 23

Ez 36:26
Moreover, I will give you a
new heart and put a new
spirit within you; and I will
remove the heart of stone
from your flesh and give
you a heart of flesh.

Mk 11:24
Therefore I say to you, all
things for which you pray
and ask, believe that you
have received them, and
they shall be granted you.

Day 24

Jer 31:34
". . . for they shall all know
Me, from the least of them
to the greatest of them,"
declares the LORD, "for I will
forgive their iniquity, and
their sin I will remember no
more."

1 Jn 5:14–15
And this is the confidence
which we have before Him,
that, if we ask anything according to His will, He hears
us. And if we know that He
hears us in whatever we
ask, we know that we have
the requests which we have
asked from Him.

Day 25
Prv 3:9–10
Honor the LORD from your
    wealth,
And from the first of all your
    produce;
So your barns will be filled
    with plenty,
And your vats will overflow
    with new wine.

Phil 4:19
And my God shall supply all
your needs according to His
riches in glory in Christ
Jesus.

Day 26
Ps 121:3
He will not allow your foot
    to slip;
He who keeps you will not
    slumber.

Heb 13:8
Jesus Christ is the same yesterday and today, yes and
forever.

Day 27
Ps 72:12
For he will deliver the
    needy when he cries for
    help,
The afflicted also, and him
    who has no helper.

1 Jn 3:22
. . . and whatever we ask
we receive from Him, be-
cause we keep His com-
mandments and do the
things that are pleasing in
His sight.

Day 28
Ps 102:17
He has regarded the prayer
    of the destitute,
And has not despised their
    prayer.

Phil 3:20–21
For our citizenship is in
heaven, from which also we
eagerly wait for a Savior,
the Lord Jesus Christ; who
will transform the body of
our humble state into con-
formity with the body of His
glory, by the exertion of the
power that He has even to
subject all things to Himself.

Day 29

Ps 9:8

And He will judge the world
   in righteousness;
He will execute judgment
   for the peoples with
   equity.

2 Pt 3:13

But according to His
promise we are looking for
new heavens and a new
earth, in which righteousness dwells.

Day 30

Jer 32:27

Behold, I am the LORD, the
God of all flesh; is anything
too difficult for Me?

2 Cor 1:20

For as many as may be the
promises of God, in Him
they are yes.

Day 31

Jer 29:12–13

Then you will call upon Me
and come and pray to Me,
and I will listen to you. And
you will seek Me and find
Me, when you search for Me
with all your heart.

Mt 7:7–8

Ask, and it shall be given to
you; seek, and you shall
find; knock, and it shall be
opened to you. For every-
one who asks receives, and
he who seeks finds, and to
him who knocks it shall be
opened.

Application C

Intercessory Prayers

Substitute your name, or the name of a friend or group, and pray these Scriptures in your own words. Pray them in the morning and evening.

Ephesians 1:17-20 Prayer

. . . that the God of our Lord Jesus Christ, the Father of glory, may give to ———— a spirit of wisdom and of revelation in the knowledge of Him. I pray that the eyes of ———— heart may be enlightened, so that ———— may know what is the hope of His calling, what are the riches of the glory of His inheritance in the saints, and what is the surpassing greatness of His power toward ———— who believe(s). These are in accordance with the working of the strength of His might which He brought about in Christ, when He raised Him from the dead, and seated Him at His right hand in heavenly places.

Ephesians 3:14-21 Prayer

For this reason, I bow my knees before the Father, from whom every family in heaven and on earth derives its name, that He would grant ————, according to the riches of His glory, to be strengthened with power through His Spirit in the inner (wo)man; so that Christ may dwell in ———— heart(s) through faith; and that ————, being rooted and grounded in love, may be able to comprehend with all the saints what is the breadth and length and height and depth, and to know the love of Christ which surpasses knowledge, that ———— may be filled up to all the fulness of God. Now to Him who is able to do exceeding abundantly beyond all that ———— ask(s) or think(s), according to the power that works within ————, to Him be the glory in the church and in Christ Jesus to all generations forever and ever. Amen.

Philippians 1:9-11 Prayer

And this I pray, that ———'s love may abound still more and more in real knowledge and all discernment, so that ——— may approve the things that are excellent, in order to be sincere and blameless until the day of Christ; having been filled with the fruit of righteousness which comes through Jesus Christ, to the glory and praise of God.

Colossians 1:9-12 Prayer

For this reason also, since the day we heard of it, we have not ceased to pray for ——— and to ask that ——— may be filled with the knowledge of His will in all spiritual wisdom and understanding, so that ——— may walk in a manner worthy of the Lord, to please Him in all respects, bearing fruit in every good work and increasing in the knowledge of God; strengthened with all power, according to His glorious might, for the attaining of all steadfastness and patience; joyously giving thanks to the Father, who has qualified ——— to share in the inheritance of the saints in light.

1 Thessalonians 3:12-13 and 5:23 Prayer

. . . and may the Lord cause ——— to increase and abound in love for one another, and for all men, just as we also do for ———; so that He may establish ——— heart(s) unblamable in holiness before our God and Father at the coming of our Lord Jesus with all His saints.

Now may the God of peace Himself sanctify ——— entirely; and may ——— spirit and soul and body be preserved complete, without blame at the coming of our Lord Jesus Christ.

Application D

Letting God Do It

Emphasis is added to the following Bible passages to illustrate how God cares for us.

Ex 14:14
The LORD *will fight for you* while you keep silent.

Dt 4:37
And He personally brought you from Egypt by His great power.

Dt 31:3, 8
It is *the LORD* your God who *will cross ahead of you; He will destroy* these nations before you, and you shall dispossess them.
And *the LORD is the one who goes ahead of you;* He will be with you. He will not fail you or forsake you. Do not fear, or be dismayed.

Jos 10:14
. . . for *the LORD fought* for Israel.

1 Sm 17:47
. . . for *the battle is the LORD's and he will give you into our hands.*

2 Chr 20:12
For we are powerless . . . our *eyes are on Thee.*

2 Chr 20:15
Do not fear or be dismayed because of this great multitude, *for the battle is not yours but God's.*

Ps 30:7

O LORD, *by Thy favor* Thou hast made my mountain to stand strong.

Ps 34:7

The angel of the LORD encamps around those who fear Him, And *rescues them.*

Ps 35:1

Contend, *O LORD,* with those who contend with me; *Fight against them who fight against me.*

Ps 37:5

Commit your way to the LORD, Trust also in Him, and *He will do it.*

Ps 39:9

I have become dumb, I do not open my mouth,
Because it is *Thou* who *hast done it.*

Ps 44:3

For by their own sword they did not possess the land;
And their own arm did not save them;
But Thy right hand, and Thine arm, and the light of Thy
    presence,
For *Thou didst favor them.*

Ps 46:10

Cease striving and know that I am God.

Ps 52:9

I will give Thee thanks forever, *because Thou hast done it.*

Ps 57:2

I will cry to the *God* Most High,
To God who *accomplishes all things* for me.

Ps 60:12

Through God we shall do valiantly,
And it is *He* who *will tread down our adversaries.*

Ps 72:18
Blessed be the Lord God, the God of Israel,
Who *alone works wonders.*

Ps 91:15
He will call upon Me, and I will answer him;
I will be with him in trouble;
I will rescue him, and honor him.

Ps 108:12
Oh give us help against the adversary,
For *deliverance by man is in vain.*

Ps 108:13
Through God we shall do valiantly;
And it is *He* who *will tread down our adversaries.*

Ps 109:27
And let them know that this is Thy hand;
Thou, Lord, *hast done it.*

Ps 127:1–2
Unless *the Lord builds the house,*
They labor in vain who build it;
Unless *the Lord guards the city,*
The watchman keeps awake in vain.
It is vain for you to rise up early,
To retire late,
To eat the bread of painful labors;
For *He gives to His beloved* even in his sleep.

Ps 138:8
The Lord will accomplish what concerns me.

Prv 21:31
The horse is prepared for the day of battle,
But *victory belongs to the Lord.*

Is 9:7
The *zeal of the Lord* of hosts *will accomplish this.*

Is 26:12
> L ord, Thou wilt establish peace for us,
> Since *Thou hast* also *performed for us all our works.*

Is 64:4
> Neither has the eye seen a God besides Thee,
> Who *acts in behalf of the one who waits for Him.*

Acts 19:11
> And *God was performing* extraordinary *miracles* by the hands of Paul.

Rom 8:3
> For what the Law could not do, weak as it was through the flesh, *God did:* sending His own Son in the likeness of sinful flesh and as an offering for sin, He condemned sin in the flesh.

1 Cor 3:7
> So then neither the one who plants nor the one who waters is anything, but *God* who *causes* the *growth.*

Col 1:12
> . . . giving thanks to *the Father,* who has *qualified us to share in the inheritance* of the saints in light.

Application E

Personalized Psalm 121

Substitute your name or a pronoun for your name and pray this psalm.

———— will lift up ———— eyes to the mountains;
From whence shall ———— come?
———— help comes from the Lord,
Who made heaven and earth.
He will not allow ———— foot to slip;
He who keeps ———— will not slumber.
Behold, He who keeps ————
Will neither slumber nor sleep.
The Lord is ———— keeper;
The Lord is ———— shade on ———— right hand.
The sun will not smite ———— by day,
Nor the moon by night.
The Lord will protect ———— from all evil;
He will keep ———— soul.
The Lord will guard ———— going out and ———— coming in
From this time forth and forever.

Application F

Jesus' Dependency on the Father's Initiative

The following selections from the Gospel of John denote Jesus' dependency on the Father, underscoring our need to trust in him:

5:30   I can do nothing on My own initiative.

8:28   I do nothing on My own initiative, but I speak these things as the Father taught Me.

8:42   . . . for I have not even come on My own initiative, but He sent Me.

12:49   For I did not speak on My own initiative, but the Father Himself who sent Me has given me commandment.

14:10   The words that I say to you I do not speak on My own initiative, but the Father abiding in Me does His works.

Application G

Twenty Insights

"Abide in Me, and I in you. As the branch cannot bear fruit of itself, unless it abides in the vine, so neither can you, unless you abide in Me. I am the vine, you are the branches; he who abides in Me, and I in Him, he bears much fruit; for apart from Me you can do nothing" (Jn 15:4–5).

1.
2.
3.
4.
5.
6.
7.
8.
9.
10.
11.
12.
13.
14.
15.
16.
17.
18.
19.
20.

Application H

Double-Entry Notebook

Practice Notebook

In the right column write what the following verses from Psalm 34 (1–3, 8–9, 22) mean to you. You may write your reaction as a narrative, poem, screenplay, letter, or whatever form you wish. Use the example notebook at the end of this application to aid you in your writing.

Entry	Reaction
I will bless the LORD at all times;	
His praise shall continually be in my mouth.	
My soul shall make its boast in the LORD;	
The humble shall hear it and rejoice.	
O magnify the LORD with me,	
And let us exalt His name together.	
O taste and see that the LORD is good;	
How blessed is the man who takes refuge in Him!	
O fear the LORD, you His saints;	
For to those who fear Him, there is no want.	
The LORD redeems the soul of His servants;	
And none of those who take refuge in Him will be condemned.	

Example Notebook

Entry	Reaction
Psalm 119:97–104	**Writer's Reaction**

Psalm 119:97–104
O how I love Thy Law!
It is my meditation all the
 day.
Thy commandments make
 me wiser than my ene-
 mies,
For they are ever mine.
I have more insight than all
 my teachers,
For Thy testimonies are my
 meditation.
I understand more than the
 aged,
Because I have observed
 Thy precepts.
I have restrained my feet
 from every evil way,
That I may keep Thy word.
I have not turned aside from
 Thine ordinances,
For Thou Thyself hast
 taught me.
How sweet are Thy words
 to my taste!
Yes, sweeter than honey to
 my mouth!
From Thy precepts I get
 understanding;
Therefore I hate every false
 way.

Writer's Reaction
Yes, Lord, I love Your word.
I want to think about it, and
think in it, and be submerged
in it constantly. For Your
word (statutes, testimonies,
commandments) make me
wise to the ways of the evil
one. They are constantly in
the forefront of my thinking
and an integral part of my
meditation. Because of your
word in my heart and mind,
I have an understanding
beyond that of a man older
than myself.

Also, meditation on your
word restrains me when I
would do evil.

Lord, help me to never turn
from your word. Your words
are as honey to my lips.
Your word gives me under-
standing to the point that I
cannot stand anything that is
false or untrue. May it ever
be so.

Application I

Scriptures to Meditate Upon

Portions of Scripture passages are provided below to aid you
in selecting passages for meditation.

Hebrew Scriptures

Gn 1:1–13   In the beginning God created the heavens and
               the earth. . . .
Lv 26:11–13   Moreover, I will make My dwelling among
               you. . . .
Dt 1:29–31   . . . God . . . fight on your behalf . . .
Dt 7:7–9   . . . God . . . keeps His covenant . . .
Dt 32:10–14   . . . The LORD alone guided him . . .
Jos 1:7–8   . . . you shall meditate on it day and night . . .
1 Kgs 19:9–12 . . . a sound of gentle blowing.
2 Chr 1:7–12   . . . Ask what I shall give you. . . .
Jb 42:1–6   . . . Thou canst do all things . . .
Ps 1:2   And in His law he meditates day and night.
Prv 4:20–27   My son, give attention to my words. . . .
Is 40:1–8   . . . the word of our God stands forever.
Is 41:10–13   Do not fear, for I am with you. . . .
Is 53:1–12   . . . He was crushed for our iniquities. . . .
Is 55:1–13   . . . For My thoughts are not your thoughts. . . .
Jer 29:11–13   For I know the plans that I have for you. . . .
Lam 3:22–33   . . . For His compassions never fail. . . .
Ez 36:24–26   For I will . . . gather you from all the lands . . .
Hos 11:1–4   . . . And out of Egypt I called My son. . . .
Mi 6:8   . . . And what does the LORD require of you . . .
Zep 3:14–17   . . . The LORD your God is in your midst. . . .

Christian Scriptures

Mt 5:1–16	. . . Blessed are the poor in spirit . . .
Mt 7:7–11	Ask, and it shall be given to you. . . .
Mt 11:28–30	Come to Me . . .
Mt 14:22–33	. . . You are certainly God's Son!
Mk 1:40–45	. . . If You are willing, You can . . .
Mk 10:13–16	. . . Permit the children to come to Me. . . .
Lk 2:1–14	Now it came about in those days . . .
Lk 7:36–50	. . . Your faith has saved you; go in peace.
Lk 18:9–14	. . . God, be merciful to me, the sinner! . . .
Lk 18:35–43	. . . Receive your sight; your faith has made you well. . . .
Lk 24:1–13	. . . He has risen. . . .
Jn 1:1–13	In the beginning was the Word. . . .
Jn 1:35–39	. . . Behold, the Lamb of God! . . .
Jn 17:1–26	These things Jesus spoke. . . .
Rom 5:1–11	Therefore having been justified by faith . . .
Rom 8:31–39	. . . If God is for us, who is against us? . . .
1 Cor 13:1–13	If I speak . . . but do not have love . . .
Eph 6:10–20	Finally, be strong in the Lord. . . .
Phil 2:5–11	Have this attitude in yourselves. . . .
Jas 1:1–8	Consider it all joy . . . when you encounter . . .
1 Jn 4:7–21	Beloved, let us love one another. . . .

Application J

Parables Found in Three Gospels

Parable	Matthew	Mark	Luke
The Lamp under a Bushel Basket	5:15	4:21	11:33
The Unshrunken Cloth	9:16	2:21	5:36
The New Wine in Old Wineskins	9:17	2:22	5:37–38
The Sower	13:3–9	4:3–8	8:5–8
The Mustard Seed	13:31–32	4:30–32	13:18–19
The Tenants	21:33–40	12:1–9	20:9–16
The Fig Tree	24:32	13:28	21:29–30

Application K

Questions Jesus Still Asks Us

Emphasis is added to the following Bible passages to under-score the specific questions Jesus still asks us.

Gospel of Matthew

6:30   *"But if God so arrays the grass of the field, which is alive today and tomorrow is thrown into the furnace, will He not much more do so for you, O men of little faith?"*

8:26   And He said to them, *"Why are you timid, you men of little faith?"* Then He arose, and rebuked the winds and the sea; and it became perfectly calm.

16:15   He said to them, *"But who do you say that I am?"*

26:40   And He came to the disciples and found them sleeping, and said to Peter, *"So you men could not keep watch with Me for one hour?"*

27:46   And about the ninth hour Jesus cried out with a loud voice, saying, "Eli, Eli, Lama Sabachthani?" that is, *"My God, My God, why hast Thou forsaken Me?"*

Gospel of Mark

2:8   And immediately Jesus, aware in His spirit that they were reasoning that way within themselves, said to them, *"Why are you reasoning about these things in your hearts?"*

3:33   And answering them, He said, *"Who are My mother and My brothers?"*

8:21   [After feeding the five thousand] And He was saying, to them *"Do you not yet understand?"*

10:18   And Jesus said to him, *"Why do you call me good?* No one is good except God alone."

12:37   *"David himself calls Him 'Lord'; and so in what sense is He his son?"* And the great crowd enjoyed listening to Him.

Gospel of Luke

6:41   *"And why do you look at the speck that is in your brother's eye, but do not notice the log that is in your own eye?"*

6:46   *"And why do you call Me, 'Lord, Lord,' and do not do what I say?'"*

7:31   *"To what then shall I compare the men of this generation, and what are they like?"*

8:25   And He said to them, *"Where is your faith?"* And they were fearful and amazed, saying to one another, "Who then is this, that He commands even the winds and the water, and they obey Him?"

14:3   And Jesus answered and spoke to the lawyers and Pharisees, saying, *"Is it lawful to heal on the Sabbath, or not?"*

Gospel of John

6:67   Jesus said therefore to the twelve, *"You do not want to go away also, do you?"*

9:35   Jesus heard that they had put him out; and finding him, He said, *"Do you believe in the Son of Man?"*

11:26   ". . . and everyone who lives and believes in Me shall never die. *Do you believe this?"*

13:12   And so when He had washed their feet, and taken His garments, and reclined at the table again, He said to them, *"Do you know what I have done to you?"*

21:17   He said to him the third time, "Simon, son of John, do you love Me?" Peter was grieved because He said to him the third time, *"Do you love Me?"* And he said to Him, "Lord, You know all things; You know that I love You." Jesus said to him, "Tend My sheep."

Application L

Seventy Forms of Prayer Writing

1. abstract
2. advertisement
3. analysis
4. anecdote
5. article
6. biography
7. book
8. brief
9. brochure
10. bulletin
11. characterization
12. children's story
13. chronicle
14. comic strip
15. composition
16. confession
17. correspondence
18. diary
19. digest
20. directory
21. drama
22. editorial
23. epic
24. episode
25. essay
26. fable
27. feature story
28. folk tale
29. glossary
30. guide
31. headline
32. humor
33. hymn
34. journal
35. lampoon
36. leaflet
37. letter (personal)
38. letter to editor
39. lexicon
40. lyrics
41. magazine article
42. manual
43. manuscript
44. memorandum
45. news story
46. note
47. novella
48. obituary
49. opus
50. pamphlet
51. picture book
52. play
53. prayer
54. proverb
55. prose
56. quotation
57. reader's theatre script
58. résumé
59. review
60. saga
61. script
62. sermon
63. speech
64. summary
65. synopsis
66. tale
67. theme
68. theses
69. tract
70. treatise

Application M

When You Do Not Have Time to Pray—Pray All Day

For some people it is impossible to find an hour in the day or night that can be spent in prayer. If this is a problem for you, try praying all day. No, this is not a malapropian clause. Here is how you can do this impossible task:

Step 1:
Read an action event from the Gospel of Mark. There are a number from which to choose. One of my favorites is the story of Legion, the man with many demons that Jesus sent out of him into a herd of swine (Mk 5:1–20). In that same chapter is the story of the woman with a twelve-year hemorrhage of blood (verses 25–34). After you have chosen and read an event, go to the next step.

Step 2:
Read the story slowly and carefully at least four more times. Take time to notice specific details.

Step 3:
Write out the sequence and repeat the story to yourself in your own words until you are thoroughly familiar with the event.

Step 4:
Write down the reference to the passage on a small piece of paper and put it in a pocket in which you often put your hand, or in a pocketbook or change purse. Or make a wrist band of paper with the verse written on it, so you will often be reminded of the passage. A precedent for this kind of reminder was set by Solomon who suggested that the commandments be bound on our fingers (Prv 7:3).

Step 5:

Whenever you see or feel the paper with the verse inscribed upon it—at the drinking fountain, a stoplight, or in light conversation—run the scene through your mind as a prayer. By the end of the week you will find that the Lord has communicated various truths to you and you will have found time for prayer.

Application N

Script Writing: The Last Five Days of Jesus Christ

The Last Five Days of Jesus Christ

Episode 4
Matthew 26:47–56

[Theme music/Breakout]
[Night sounds of crickets, shuffling feet, soldiers' swords clanking, etc.]
NARRATOR: At the moment Jesus was speaking to his disciples, Judas, one of the twelve, came up to Jesus. Behind Judas was a great multitude with swords and clubs. They were from the chief priests and elders of the people. Judas speaks.
  [The night sounds grow louder at this point and the frightened voices of the disciples are heard in the background]
JUDAS: Whomever I shall kiss, He is the one; seize Him.
NARRATOR: Judas moves directly into the path of Jesus and says,
JUDAS: Hail, Rabbi!
NARRATOR: Judas leans forward and kisses Jesus on the cheek. Jesus says quietly,
JESUS: Friend, do what you have come for.
  [Scuffling, shouting, and the ominous swish of a sword blade cutting flesh and a soldier crying out in pain]
SOLDIER: My ear, my ear, he cut off my ear!
JESUS: Put your sword back into its place. . . .

Application O

Written Confession

On a separate sheet of paper, list your sins.

Next, substitute your name, or a pronoun for your name (I, my, me) in the blank spaces of 1 John 1:9 below. Repeat this verse in your own words until you sense God dwelling in your life.

If ——— confess ——— sins, He is faithful and righteous to forgive ——— sins and to cleanse ——— from all unrighteousness.

Now, destroy the copy of your confessed sins.

Application P

Love

1 Corinthians 13:4-8

———— is patient, ————is kind, and
———— is not jealous;
———— does not brag and
———— is not arrogant,
———— does not act unbecomingly;
———— does not seek ————'s own,
———— is not provoked,
———— does not take into account a wrong suffered,
———— does not rejoice in unrighteousness, but
———— rejoices with the truth;
———— bears all things,
———— believes all things,
———— hopes all things,
———— endures all things.
———— never fails. . . .

Read the text above, inserting the word *love* in each of the blanks. Read the text again, inserting your name in the blanks, and pray-write your answers to the following statements:

1. My first reaction is ————.
2. The emotions I feel as I pray-write this text are ————.
3. The most important word and/or phrase in the text is ———— because ————.
4. The text connects my mind with other Scriptures and biblical personalities such as ———— and leads me to pray that ————.

Reference List

Barry, William A. 1987. *God and You: Prayer as a Personal Relationship.* Mahwah, N.J.: Paulist Press.

———. 1989. *Seek My Face: Prayer as Personal Relationship in Scripture.* Mahwah, N.J.: Paulist Press.

Bartlett, John. 1968. *Familiar Quotations: A Collection of Passages, Phrases and Proverbs Tracked to Their Sources in Ancient and Modern Literature.* 14th ed. Boston, Mass.: Little, Brown and Company.

Berthoff, Ann E. 1981. *The Making of Meaning: Metaphors, Models, and Maxims for Writing Teachers.* Upper Montclair, N.J.: Boynton/Cook Publishers.

Billheimer, Paul E. 1975. *Destined for the Throne.* Minneapolis, Minn.: Bethany House Publishers.

Boase, Leonard. 1985. *The Prayer of Faith.* Chicago: Loyola University Press.

Bozzi, Vincent. 1988. "A Healthy Dose of Religion." *Psychology Today* 22 (November): 14–15.

Canham, Elizabeth. 1987. *Praying the Bible: A Parish Life Sourcebook.* Cambridge, Mass.: Cowley Publications.

Cheyney, Arnold B. 1982. *The Poetry Corner.* Glenview, Ill.: Scott, Foresman and Company.

Dembo, Myron H. 1988. *Applying Educational Psychology in the Classroom.* 3rd ed. New York: Longman.

Dunn, Ronald. 1991. *Don't Just Stand There, Pray Something: The Incredible Power of Intercessory Prayer.* San Bernardino, Calif.: Here's Life Publishers, Inc.

Eastman, Dick. 1978. *The Hour That Changes the World: A Practical Handbook for Personal Prayer.* Grand Rapids, Mich.: Baker Book House.

Emig, Janet. 1983. *The Web of Meaning: Essays on Writing, Teaching, Learning, and Thinking.* Upper Montclair, N.J.: Boynton/Cook Publishers.

Foster, Richard J. 1992. *Prayer: Finding the Heart's True Home.* San Francisco: Harper San Francisco.

Groeschel, Benedict J. 1984. *Listening at Prayer.* Mahwah, N.J.: Paulist Press.

Hallesby, O. 1975. *Prayer.* Minneapolis, Minn.: Augsburg Publishing House.

Hassel, David J. 1984. *Radical Prayer: Creating a Welcome for God, Ourselves, Other People and the World.* Ramsey, N. J.: Paulist Press.

Hunt, Dave, and T. A. McMahon. 1985. *The Seduction of Christianity: Spiritual Discernment in the Last Days.* Eugene, Ore.: Harvest House Publishers.

Jäger, Willigis. 1986. *The Way of Contemplation: Encountering God Today.* Mahwah, N.J.: Paulist Press.

Langer, Judith A., and Arthur N. Applebee. 1987. *How Writing Shapes Thinking: A Study of Teaching and Learning.* Urbana, Ill.: National Council of Teachers of English.

Lea, Larry. 1987. *Could You Not Tarry One Hour?* Altamonte Springs, Fla.: Creation House.

Leggett, Glenn, C. David Mead, and Melinda G. Kramer. 1991. *Prentice-Hall Handbook for Writers.* 11th ed. Englewood Cliffs, N.J.: Prentice-Hall.

Lockyer, Herbert. 1962. *All the Promises of the Bible.* Grand Rapids, Mich.: Zondervan Publishing House.

Macrorie, Ken. 1984. *Writing to Be Read.* Rev. 3rd ed. Upper Montclair, N.J.: Boynton/Cook Publishers.

McQuilkin, Robertson. 1992. *Understanding and Applying the Bible.* Chicago: Moody Press.

Merton, Thomas. 1961. *New Seeds of Contemplation.* New York: New Directions Book.

Montessori, Maria. 1967. *The Montessori Method: Scientific Pedagogy as Applied to Child Education in the "Children's Houses."* Trans. Anne E. George. Cambridge, Mass.: Robert Bentley.

Murray, Andrew. 1981. *The Ministry of Intercessory Prayer.* Minneapolis, Minn.: Bethany House Publishers.

Partridge, Eric. 1984. *A Dictionary of Slang and Unconventional English.* 8th ed. New York: Macmillan.

Pennebaker, James W., Janice K. Kiecolt-Glaser, and Ronald Glaser. 1988. "Disclosure of Traumas and Immune Function: Health Implications for Psychotherapy." *Journal of Consulting and Clinical Psychology* 56:239–45.

Riccio, Ottone M. 1980. *The Intimate Art of Writing Poetry.* Englewood, Cliffs, N.J.: Prentice-Hall, Inc.

Rico, Gabriele Lusser. 1983. *Writing the Natural Way: Using Right-Brain Techniques to Release Your Expressive Powers.* Los Angeles: J. P. Tarcher, Inc.

Stafford, William. 1987. *Writing the Australian Crawl.* Ann Arbor, Mich.: University of Michigan Press.

Swanson, Kenneth. 1987. *Uncommon Prayer: Approaching Intimacy with God.* New York: Ballantine.

Trueblood, Elton. 1964. *The Humor of Christ*. New York: Harper and Row.

Ulanov, Ann, and Barry Ulanov. 1982. *Primary Speech: A Psychology of Prayer*. Atlanta, Ga.: John Knox Press.

Vanderwall, Francis W. 1989. *Water in the Wilderness*. Mahwah, N.J.: Paulist Press.

Zinsser, William. 1980. *On Writing Well: An Informal Guide to Writing Nonfiction*. 2nd ed. New York: Harper and Row.

————. 1988. *Writing to Learn*. New York: Harper and Row.

Notes

Notes

Notes

Notes

Notes

Notes

Notes